UNIX® System V/386
Release 3.2
Network Programmer's Guide

Prentice Hall, Englewood Cliffs, New Jersey 07632

Library of Congress Catalog Card Number: 88-62525

Editorial/production supervision: Karen Skrable Fortgang
Manufacturing buyer: Mary Ann Gloriande

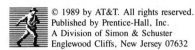
The publisher offers discounts on this book when ordered
in bulk quantities. For more information, write or call:

Special Sales
Prentice-Hall, Inc.
College Technical and Reference Division
Englewood Cliffs, NJ 07632
(201) 592-2498

Printed in the United States of America

10 9 8 7 6 5 4 3

ISBN 0-13-944935-3

Prentice-Hall International (UK) Limited, *London*
Prentice-Hall of Australia Pty. Limited, *Sydney*
Prentice-Hall Canada Inc., *Toronto*
Prentice-Hall Hispanoamericana, S.A., *Mexico*
Prentice-Hall of India Private Limited, *New Delhi*
Prentice-Hall of Japan, Inc., *Tokyo*
Simon & Schuster Asia Pte. Ltd., *Singapore*
Editora Prentice-Hall do Brasil, Ltda., *Rio de Janeiro*

Table of Contents

List of Figures

1 Introduction to the Guide

Introduction to the Guide

This document provides detailed information, with various examples, on the UNIX System Transport Interface. This guide is intended for programmers who require the services defined by this interface. Working knowledge of UNIX System programming and data communication concepts is assumed. In particular, working knowledge of the Reference Model of Open Systems Interconnection (OSI) is required.

Background

To place the Transport Interface in perspective, a discussion of the OSI Reference Model is first presented. The Reference Model partitions networking functions into seven layers, as depicted in Figure 1-1.

Layer 7	application
Layer 6	presentation
Layer 5	session
Layer 4	transport
Layer 3	network
Layer 2	data link
Layer 1	physical

Figure 1-1: OSI Reference Model

Layer 1   The physical layer is responsible for the transmission of raw data over a communication medium.

Layer 2   The data link layer provides the exchange of data between network layer entities. It detects and corrects any errors that may occur in the physical layer transmission.

Layer 3   The network layer manages the operation of the network. In particular, it is responsible for the routing and management of data exchange between transport layer entities within the network.

Layer 4   The transport layer provides transparent data transfer services between session layer entities by relieving them from concerns of how reliable and cost-effective transfer of data is achieved.

Layer 5   The session layer provides the services needed by presentation layer entities that enable them to organize and synchronize their dialogue and manage their data exchange.

Layer 6   The presentation layer manages the representation of information that application layer entities either communicate or reference in their communication.

Layer 7   The application layer serves as the window between corresponding application processes that are exchanging information.

A basic principle of the Reference Model is that each layer provides services needed by the next higher layer in a way that frees the upper layer from concern about how these services are provided. This approach simplifies the design of each particular layer.

Industry standards either have been or are being defined at each layer of the Reference Model. Two standards are defined at each layer: one that specifies an interface to the services of the layer, and one that defines the protocol by which services are provided. A service interface standard at any layer frees users of the service from details of how that layer's protocol is implemented, or even which protocol is used to provide the service.

The transport layer is important because it is the lowest layer in the Reference Model that provides the basic service of reliable, end-to-end data transfer needed by applications and higher layer protocols. In doing so, this layer hides the topology and characteristics of the underlying network from its users. More important, however, the transport layer defines a set of services common to layers of many contemporary protocol suites, including the International Standards Organization (ISO) protocols, the Transmission Control Protocol and Internet Protocol (TCP/IP) of the ARPANET, Xerox Network Systems (XNS), and the Systems Network Architecture (SNA).

A transport service interface, then, could enable applications and higher layer protocols to be implemented without knowledge of the underlying protocol suite. That is a principle goal of the UNIX System Transport Interface. Also, because an inherent characteristic of the transport layer is that it hides details of the physical medium being used, the Transport Interface offers both protocol and medium independence to networking applications and higher layer protocols.

The UNIX System Transport Interface was modeled after the industry standard ISO Transport Service Definition (ISO 8072). As such, it is intended for those applications and protocols that require transport services. It is not intended to provide a generic networking interface for all UNIX System applications, but is a first step in providing networking services with UNIX System V/386. Because the Transport Interface provides reliable data transfer, and because its services are common to several protocol suites, many networking applications will find these services useful.

The Transport Interface is implemented as a user library using the STREAMS input/output (I/O) mechanism. Therefore, many services available to STREAMS applications are also available to users of the Transport Interface. These services will be highlighted throughout this guide. The *STREAMS Primer* and *STREAMS Programmer's Guide* contain more detailed information on STREAMS for the interested reader.

Document Organization

This guide is organized as follows:

■ Chapter 2, "Overview of the Transport Interface," summarizes the basic set of services available to Transport Interface users and presents the background information needed for the remainder of the guide.

■ Chapter 3, "Connection-Mode Service," describes the services associated with connection-based (or virtual circuit) communication.

■ Chapter 4, "Connectionless-Mode Service," describes the services associated with connectionless (or datagram) communication.

■ Chapter 5, "A Read/Write Interface," describes how users can use the services of **read** [see *read*(2)] and **write** [see *write*(2)] to communicate over transport connection.

■ Chapter 6, "Advanced Topics," discusses important concepts that are not covered in earlier chapters. These include asynchronous event handling and processing of multiple, simultaneous connect requests.

■ Appendix A, "State Transitions," defines the allowable state transitions associated with the Transport Interface.

■ Appendix B, "Guidelines for Protocol Independence," establishes necessary guidelines for developing software that may run without change over any transport protocol developed for the Transport Interface.

■ Appendix C, "Examples," presents the full listing of each programming example used throughout the guide.

■ The Glossary defines Transport Interface terms and acronyms used in this guide.

This guide describes the more important and common facilities of the Transport Interface and is not meant to be exhaustive. Section 3N of the *Programmer's Reference Manual* contains a complete description of each Transport Interface routine.

Notational Conventions

The following notational conventions are used throughout this *Guide*:

bold	User input, such as commands, options to commands, and the names of directories and files, appear in **bold**.
italic	Names of variables to which values must be assigned (such as *filename*) appear in *italic*.
command(number)	A command name followed by a number in parentheses refers to the part of a UNIX system reference manual that documents that command. (There are two reference manuals: the *User's/System Administrator's Reference Manual* and the *Programmer's Reference Manual*.) For example, the notation *cat*(1) refers to the page in section 1 (of the *User's/System Administrator's Reference Manual*) that documents the **cat** command.

`constant width`   UNIX System output, such as prompt signs and
                          responses to commands, and program examples
                          appear in `constant width`.

2 Overview of the Transport Interface

Introduction

This chapter presents a high-level overview of the services of the Transport Interface, which supports the transfer of data between two user processes. Figure 2-1 illustrates the Transport Interface.

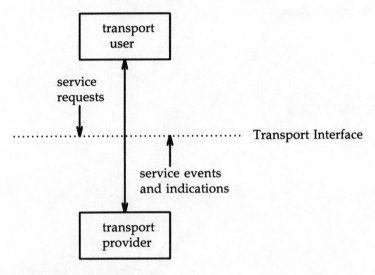

Figure 2-1: Transport Interface

The transport provider is the entity that provides the services of the Transport Interface, and the transport user is the entity that requires these services. An example of a transport provider is the ISO transport protocol, while a transport user may be a networking application or session layer protocol.

The transport user accesses the services of the transport provider by issuing the appropriate service requests. One example is a request to transfer data over a connection. Similarly, the transport provider notifies the user of various events, such as the arrival of data on a connection.

The Network Services Library of UNIX System V/386 includes a set of functions that support the services of the Transport Interface for user processes [see *intro*(3)]. These functions enable a user to initiate requests to the provider and process incoming events. Programs using the Transport Interface can link the appropriate routines as follows:

    cc prog.c -lnsl_s

Modes of Service

Two modes of service, connection-mode and connectionless-mode, are provided by the Transport Interface. Connection-mode is circuit-oriented and enables data to be transmitted over an established connection in a reliable, sequenced manner. It also provides an identification mechanism that avoids the overhead of address resolution and transmission during the data transfer phase. This service is attractive for applications that require relatively long-lived, datastream-oriented interactions.

Connectionless-mode, in contrast, is message-oriented and supports data transfer in self-contained units with no logical relationship required among multiple units. This service requires only a preexisting association between the peer users involved, which determines the characteristics of the data to be transmitted. All the information required to deliver a unit of data (for example, the destination address) is presented to the transport provider, together with the data to be transmitted, in one service access (which need not relate to any other service access). Each unit of data transmitted is entirely self-contained. Connectionless-mode service is attractive for applications that:

■ involve short-term request/response interactions

■ exhibit a high level of redundancy

■ are dynamically reconfigurable

■ do not require guaranteed in-sequence delivery of data

Connection-Mode Service

The connection-mode transport service is characterized by four phases: local management, connection establishment, data transfer, and connection release.

Local Management

The local management phase defines local operations between a transport user and a transport provider. For example, a user must establish a channel of communication with the transport provider, as illustrated in Figure 2-2. Each channel between a transport user and transport provider is a unique endpoint of communication, and will be called the transport endpoint. The t_open routine enables a user to choose a particular transport provider that will supply the connection-mode services, and establishes the transport endpoint.

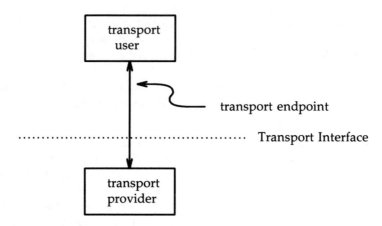

Figure 2-2: Channel Between User and Provider

Another necessary local function for each user is to establish an identity with the transport provider. Each user is identified by a transport address. More accurately, a transport address is associated with each transport endpoint, and one user process may manage several transport endpoints. In connection-mode service, one user requests a connection to another user by specifying that user's address. The structure of a transport address is defined by the address space of the transport provider. An address may be as simple as a random character string (for example, "file_server"), or as complex as an encoded bit pattern that specifies all information needed to route data through a network. Each transport provider defines its own mechanism or identifying users. Addresses may be assigned to each transport endpoint by **t_bind**.

In addition to **t_open** and **t_bind**, several routines are available to support local operations. Figure 2-3 summarizes all local management routines of the Transport Interface.

Command	Description
t_alloc	Allocates Transport Interface data structures [see *t_alloc*(3N)].
t_bind	Binds a transport address to a transport endpoint [see *t_bind*(3N)].
t_close	Closes a transport endpoint [see *t_close*(3N)].
t_error	Prints a Transport Interface error message [see *t_error*(3N)].
t_free	Frees structures allocated using **t_alloc** [see *t_free*(3N)].
t_getinfo	Returns a set of parameters associated with a particular transport provider [see *t_getinfo*(3N)].
t_getstate	Returns the state of a transport endpoint [see *t_getstate*(3N)].
t_look	Returns the current event on a transport endpoint [see *t_look*(3N)].
t_open	Establishes a transport endpoint connected to a chosen transport provider [see *t_open*(3N)].
t_optmgmt	Negotiates protocol-specific options with the transport provider [see *t_optmgmt*(3N)].
t_sync	Synchronizes a transport endpoint with the transport provider [see *t_sync*(3N)].
t_unbind	Unbinds a transport address from a transport endpoint [see *t_unbind*(3N)].

Figure 2-3: Local Management Routines

Connection Establishment

The connection establishment phase enables two users to create a connection, or virtual circuit, between them, as demonstrated in Figure 2-4.

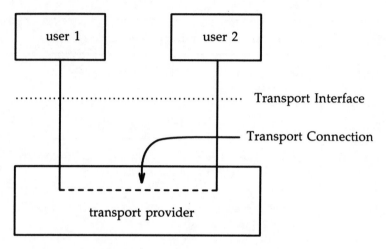

Figure 2-4: Transport Connection

This phase is illustrated by a client/server relationship between two transport users. One user, the server, typically advertises some service to a group of users, and then listens for requests from those users. As each client requires the service, it attempts to connect itself to the server using the server's advertised transport address. The **t_connect** routine initiates the connect request. One argument to **t_connect**, the transport address, identifies the server the client wishes to access. The server is notified of each incoming request using **t_listen**, and may call **t_accept** to accept the client's request for access to the service. If the request is accepted, the transport connection is established.

Figure 2-5 summarizes all routines available for establishing a transport connection.

Command	Description
t_accept	Accepts a request for a transport connection [see *t_accept*(3N)].
t_connect	Establishes a connection with the transport user at a specified destination [see *t_connect*(3N)].
t_listen	Retrieves an indication of a connect request from another transport user [see *t_listen*(3N)].
t_rcvconnect	Completes connection establishment if **t_connect** was called in asynchronous mode (see Chapter 6) [see *t_rcvconnect*(3N)].

Figure 2-5: Connection Establishment Routines

Data Transfer

The data transfer phase enables users to transfer data in both directions over an established connection. Two routines, **t_snd** and **t_rcv**, send and receive data over this connection. All data sent by a user is guaranteed to be delivered to the user on the other end of the connection in the order in which it was sent. Figure 2-6 summarizes the connection-mode data transfer routines.

Command	Description
t_rcv	Retrieves data that has arrived over a transport connection [see *t_rcv*(3N)].
t_snd	Sends data over an established transport connection [see *t_snd*(3N)].

Figure 2-6: Connection-Mode Data Transfer Routines

Connection Release

The connection release phase provides a mechanism for breaking an established connection. When you decide that the conversation should terminate, you can request that the provider release the transport connection. Two types of connection release are supported by the Transport Interface. The first is an abortive release, which directs the transport provider to release the connection immediately. Any previously sent data that has not yet reached the other transport user may be discarded by the transport provider. The **t_snddis** routine initiates this abortive disconnect, and **t_rcvdis** processes the incoming indication of an abortive disconnect.

All transport providers must support the abortive release procedure. In addition, some transport providers may also support an orderly release facility that enables users to terminate communication gracefully with no data loss. The functions **t_sndrel** and **t_rcvrel** support this capability. Figure 2-7 summarizes the connection release routines.

Command	Description
t_rcvdis	Returns an indication of an aborted connection, including a reason code and user data [see *t_rcvdis*(3N)].
t_rcvrel	Returns an indication that the remote user has requested an orderly release of a connection [see *t_rcvrel*(3N)].
t_snddis	Aborts a connection or rejects a connect request [see *t_snddis*(3N)].
t_sndrel	Requests the orderly release of a connection [see *t_sndrel*(3N)].

Figure 2-7: Connection Release Routines

Connectionless-Mode Service

The connectionless-mode transport service is characterized by two phases: local management and data transfer. The local management phase defines the same local operations described above for the connection-mode service.

The data transfer phase enables a user to transfer data units (sometimes called datagrams) to the specified peer user. Each data unit must be accompanied by the transport address of the destination user. Two routines, **t_sndudata** and **t_rcvudata**, support this message-based data transfer facility. Figure 2-8 summarizes all routines associated with connectionless-mode data transfer.

Command	Description
t_rcvudata	Retrieves a message sent by another transport user [see *t_rcvudata*(3N)].
t_rcvuderr	Retrieves error information associated with a previously sent message [see *t_rcvuderr*(3N)].
t_sndudata	Sends a message to the specified destination user [see *t_sndudata*(3N)].

Figure 2-8: Connectionless-Mode Data Transfer Routines

State Transitions

The Transport Interface has two components:

■ the library routines that provide the transport services to users

■ the state transition rules that define the sequence in which the transport routines may be invoked

The state transition rules are presented in Appendix A of this guide in the form of state tables. The state tables define the legal sequence of library calls based on state information and the handling of events. These events include user-generated library calls, as well as provider-generated event indications.

 NOTE Any user of the Transport Interface must completely understand all possible state transitions before writing software using the interface.

3 Connection-mode Service

Introduction

This chapter describes the connection-mode service of the Transport Interface. As discussed in the previous chapter, the connection-mode service can be illustrated using a client/server example. The important concepts of connection-mode service will be presented using two programming examples. The examples are related in that the first illustrates how a client establishes a connection to a server and then communicates with the server. The second example shows the server's side of the interaction. All examples discussed in this guide are presented in their entirety in Appendix C.

In the examples, the client establishes a connection with a server process. The server then transfers a file to the client. The client, in turn, receives the data from the server and writes it to its standard output file.

Local Management

Before the client and server can establish a transport connection, each must first establish a local channel (the transport endpoint) to the transport provider using **t_open**, and establish its identity (or address) using **t_bind**.

The set of services supported by the Transport Interface may not be implemented by all transport protocols. Each transport provider has a set of characteristics associated with it that determine the services it offers and the limitations associated with those services. This information is returned to the user by **t_open**, and consists of the following:

addr	maximum size of a transport address
options	maximum bytes of protocol-specific options that may be passed between the transport user and transport provider
tsdu	maximum message size that may be transmitted in either connection-mode or connectionless-mode
etsdu	maximum expedited data message size that may be sent over a transport connection
connect	maximum number of bytes of user data that may be passed between users during connection establishment
discon	maximum bytes of user data that may be passed between users during the abortive release of a connection
servtype	the type of service supported by the transport provider

The three service types defined by the Transport Interface are:

T_COTS	The transport provider supports connection-mode service but does not provide the optional orderly release facility.
T_COTS_ORD	The transport provider supports connection-mode service with the optional orderly release facility.
T_CLTS	The transport provider supports connectionless-mode service.

Only one such service can be associated with the transport provider identified by **t_open**.

NOTE

t_open returns the default provider characteristics associated with a transport endpoint. However, some characteristics may change after an endpoint has been opened. This will occur if the characteristics are associated with negotiated options (described later in this chapter). For example, if the support of expedited data transfer is a negotiated option, the value of this characteristic may change. **t_getinfo** may be called to retrieve the current characteristics of a transport endpoint.

Once a user establishes a transport endpoint with the chosen transport provider, it must establish its identity. As mentioned earlier, **t_bind** accomplishes this by binding a transport address to the transport endpoint. In addition, for servers, this routine informs the transport provider that the endpoint will be used to listen for incoming connect requests, also called connect indications.

An optional facility, **t_optmgmt** [see *t_optmgmt*(3N)], is also available during the local management phase. It enables a user to negotiate the values of protocol options with the transport provider. Each transport protocol is expected to define its own set of negotiable protocol options, which may include such information as Quality-of-Service parameters. Because of the protocol-specific nature of options, only applications written for a particular protocol environment are expected to use this facility.

The Client

The local management requirements of the example client and server are used to discuss details of these facilities. The following are the definitions needed by the client program, followed by its necessary local management steps.

```
#include <stdio.h>
#include <tiuser.h>
#include <fcntl.h>

#define SRV_ADDR    1    /* server's well known address */

main( )
{
    int fd;
    int nbytes;
    int flags = 0;
    char buf[1024];
    struct t_call *sndcall;
    extern int t_errno;

    if ((fd = t_open("/dev/tivc", O_RDWR, NULL)) < 0) {
        t_error("t_open failed");
        exit(1);
    }

    if (t_bind(fd, NULL, NULL) < 0) {
        t_error("t_bind failed");
        exit(2);
    }
```

The first argument to **t_open** is the path name of a file system node that identifies the transport protocol that will supply the transport service. In this example, **/dev/tivc** is a STREAMS **clone** device node that identifies a generic, connection-based transport protocol [see *clone*(7)]. The **clone** device finds an available minor device of the transport provider for the user. It is opened for both reading and writing, as specified by the O_RDWR open flag. The third argument may be used to return the service characteristics of the transport provider to the user. This information is useful when writing protocol-independent software (discussed in Appendix B). For simplicity, the client and server in this example ignore this information and assume the transport provider has the following characteristics:

- The transport address is an integer value that uniquely identifies each user.

- The transport provider supports the T_COTS_ORD service type, and the example will use the orderly release facility to release the connection.

- User data may not be passed between users during either connection establishment or abortive release.

- The transport provider does not support protocol-specific options.

Because these characteristics are not needed by the user, NULL is specified in the third argument to **t_open**. If the user needed a service other than T_COTS_ORD, another transport provider would be opened. An example of the T_CLTS service invocation is presented in Chapter 4.

The return value of **t_open** is an identifier for the transport endpoint that will be used by all subsequent Transport Interface function calls. This identifier is actually a file descriptor obtained by opening the transport protocol file [see *open*(2)]. The significance of this fact is highlighted in Chapter 5.

After the transport endpoint is created, the client calls **t_bind** to assign an address to the endpoint. The first argument identifies the transport endpoint. The second argument describes the address the user would like to bind to the endpoint, and the third argument is set on return from **t_bind** to specify the address that the provider bound.

The address associated with a server's transport endpoint is important because that is the address used by all clients to access the server. However, the typical client does not care what its own address is, because no other process will try to access it. That is the case in this example, where the second and third arguments to **t_bind** are set to NULL. A NULL second argument will direct the transport provider to choose an address for the user. A NULL third argument indicates that the user does not care what address was assigned to the endpoint.

If either **t_open** or **t_bind** fail, the program will call **t_error** [see *t_error*(3N)] to print an appropriate error message to **stderr**. If any Transport Interface routine fails, the global integer **t_errno** will be assigned an appropriate transport error value. A set of such error values has been defined (in <**tiuser.h**>) for the Transport Interface, and **t_error** will print an error message corresponding to the value in **t_errno**. This routine is analogous to **perror** [see *perror*(3C)], which prints an error message based on the value of **errno**. If the error associated with a transport function is a system error,

t_errno will be set to TSYSERR and **errno** will be set to the appropriate value.

The Server

The server in this example must take similar local management steps before communication can begin. The server must establish a transport endpoint through which it will listen for connect indications. The necessary definitions and local management steps are shown below:

```
#include <tiuser.h>
#include <stropts.h>
#include <fcntl.h>
#include <stdio.h>
#include <signal.h>


#define DISCONNECT  -1
#define SRV_ADDR     1  /* server's well-known address */


int conn_fd;            /* connection established here */
extern int t_errno;

main( )
{

   int listen_fd;       /* listening transport endpoint */
   struct t_bind *bind;
   struct t_call *call;

   if ((listen_fd = t_open("/dev/tivc", O_RDWR, NULL)) < 0) {
      t_error("t_open failed for listen_fd");
      exit(1);
   }


   /*
    * By assuming that the address is an integer value,
    * this program may not run over another protocol.
    */
```

continued

```
if ((bind = (struct t_bind *)t_alloc(listen_fd, T_BIND, T_ALL)) == NULL) {
    t_error("t_alloc of t_bind structure failed");
    exit(2);
}


bind->qlen = 1;
bind->addr.len = sizeof(int);
*(int *)bind->addr.buf = SRV_ADDR;


if (t_bind(listen_fd, bind, bind) < 0) {
    t_error("t_bind failed for listen_fd");
    exit(3);
}


/*
 * Was the correct address bound?
 */
if (*(int *)bind->addr.buf != SRV_ADDR) {
    fprintf(stderr, "t_bind bound wrong address0);
    exit(4);
}
```

As with the client, the first step is to call **t_open** to establish a transport endpoint with the desired transport provider. This endpoint, *listen_fd*, will be used to listen for connect indications. Next, the server must bind its well-known address to the endpoint. This address is used by each client to access the server. The second argument to **t_bind** requests that a particular address be bound to the transport endpoint. This argument points to a **t_bind** structure with the following format:

```
struct t_bind {
   struct netbuf addr;
   unsigned qlen;
}
```

where *addr* describes the address to be bound, and *qlen* indicates the maximum outstanding connect indications that may arrive at this endpoint. All
Transport Interface structure and constant definitions are found in <**tiuser.h**>.

The address is specified using a **netbuf** structure that contains the following members:

```
struct netbuf {
   unsigned int maxlen;
   unsigned int len;
   char *buf;
}
```

where *buf* points to a buffer containing the data, *len* specifies the bytes of data
in the buffer, and *maxlen* indicates the maximum bytes the buffer can hold
(and need only be set when data is returned to the user by a Transport Interface routine). For the **t_bind** structure, the data pointed to by *buf* identifies a
transport address. It is expected that the structure of addresses will vary
among each protocol implementation under the Transport Interface. The **netbuf** structure is intended to support any such structure.

If the value of *qlen* is greater than 0, the transport endpoint may be used
to listen for connect indications. In such cases, **t_bind** directs the transport
provider to immediately begin queueing connect indications destined for the
bound address. Furthermore, the value of *qlen* indicates the maximum outstanding connect indications the server wishes to process. The server must
respond to each connect indication, either accepting or rejecting the request
for connection. An outstanding connect indication is one to which the server
has not yet responded. Often, a server will fully process a single connect indication and respond to it before receiving the next indication. In this case, a
value of 1 is appropriate for *qlen*. However, some servers may wish to
retrieve several connect indications before responding to any of them. In such
cases, *qlen* indicates the maximum number of such outstanding indications the
server will process. An example of a server that manages multiple outstanding connect indications is presented in Chapter 6.

t_alloc is called to allocate the **t_bind** structure needed by **t_bind**. **t_alloc** takes three arguments. The first is a file descriptor that references a transport endpoint. This is used to access the characteristics of the transport provider [see *t_open*(3N)]. The second argument identifies the appropriate Transport Interface structure to be allocated. The third argument specifies which, if any, **netbuf** buffers should be allocated for that structure. T_ALL specifies that all **netbuf** buffers associated with the structure should be allocated, and will cause the *addr* buffer to be allocated in this example. The size of this buffer is determined from the transport provider characteristic that defines the maximum address size. The *maxlen* field of this **netbuf** structure will be set to the size of the newly allocated buffer by **t_alloc**. The use of **t_alloc** will help ensure the compatibility of user programs with future releases of the Transport Interface.

The server in this example will process connect indications one at a time, so *qlen* is set to one. The address information is then assigned to the newly allocated **t_bind** structure. This **t_bind** structure will be used to pass information to **t_bind** in the second argument, and also will be used to return information to the user in the third argument.

On return, the **t_bind** structure will contain the address that was bound to the transport endpoint. If the provider could not bind the requested address, perhaps because it had been bound to another transport endpoint, it will choose another appropriate address.

NOTE

Each transport provider will manage its address space differently. Some transport providers may allow a single transport address to be bound to several transport endpoints, while others may require a unique address per endpoint. The Transport Interface supports either choice. Based on its address management rules, a provider will determine if it can bind the requested address. If not, it will choose another valid address from its address space and bind it to the transport endpoint.

The server must check the bound address to ensure that it is the one previously advertised to clients. Otherwise, the clients will be unable to reach the server.

If **t_bind** succeeds, the provider will begin queueing connect indications. The next phase of communication, connection establishment, is entered.

Connection Establishment

The connection establishment procedures highlight the distinction between clients and servers. The Transport Interface imposes a different set of procedures in this phase for each type of transport user. The client initiates the connection establishment procedure by requesting a connection to a particular server using **t_connect**. The server is then notified of the client's request by calling **t_listen**. The server may either accept or reject the client's request. It will call **t_accept** to establish the connection, or call **t_snddis** to reject the request. The client will be notified of the server's decision when **t_connect** completes.

The Transport Interface supports two facilities during connection establishment that may not be supported by all transport providers. The first is the ability to transfer data between the client and server when establishing the connection. The client may send data to the server when it requests a connection. This data will be passed to the server by **t_listen**. Similarly, the server can send data to the client when it accepts or rejects the connection. The connect characteristic returned by **t_open** determines how much data, if any, two users may transfer during connect establishment.

The second optional service supported by the Transport Interface during connection establishment is the negotiation of protocol options. The client may specify protocol options that it would like the remote user and/or transport provider to use. The Transport Interface supports both local and remote option negotiation. As discussed earlier, option negotiation is inherently a protocol-specific function. Use of this facility is discouraged if protocol-independent software is a goal (see Appendix B).

The Client

Continuing with the client/server example, the steps needed by the client to establish a connection are shown next:

```
/*
 * By assuming that the address is an integer value,
 * this program may not run over another protocol.
 */
if ((sndcall = (struct t_call *)t_alloc(fd, T_CALL, T_ADDR)) == NULL) {
    t_error("t_alloc failed");
    exit(3);
}
sndcall->addr.len = sizeof(int);
*(int *)sndcall->addr.buf = SRV_ADDR;

if (t_connect(fd, sndcall, NULL) < 0) {
    t_error("t_connect failed for fd");
    exit(4);
}
```

The **t_connect** call establishes the connection with the server. The first argument to **t_connect** identifies the transport endpoint through which the connection is established, and the second argument identifies the destination server. This argument is a pointer to a **t_call** structure, which has the following format:

```
struct t_call {
    struct netbuf addr;
    struct netbuf opt;
    struct netbuf udata;
    int sequence;
}
```

addr identifies the address of the server, *opt* may be used to specify protocol-specific options that the client would like to associate with the connection, and *udata* identifies user data that may be sent with the connect request to the server. The *sequence* field has no meaning for **t_connect**.

t_alloc is called above to allocate the **t_call** structure dynamically. Once allocated, the appropriate values are assigned. In this example, no options or user data are associated with the **t_connect** call, but the server's address must be set. The third argument to **t_alloc** is set to T_ADDR to indicate that an appropriate **netbuf** buffer should be allocated for the address. The server's address is then assigned to *buf*, and *len* is set accordingly.

The third argument to **t_connect** can be used to return information about the newly established connection to the user, and may retrieve any user data sent by the server in its response to the connect request. It is set to NULL by the client here to indicate that this information is not needed. The connection will be established on successful return of **t_connect**. If the server rejects the connect request, **t_connect** will fail and set **t_errno** to TLOOK.

Event Handling

The TLOOK error has special significance in the Transport Interface. Some Transport Interface routines may be interrupted by an unexpected asynchronous transport event on the given transport endpoint, and TLOOK notifies the user that an event has occurred. As such, TLOOK does not indicate an error with a Transport Interface routine, but the normal processing of that routine will not be performed because of the pending event. The events defined by the Transport Interface are listed here:

T_LISTEN	A request for a connection, called a connect indication, has arrived at the transport endpoint.
T_CONNECT	The confirmation of a previously sent connect request, called a connect confirmation, has arrived at the transport endpoint. The confirmation is generated when a server accepts a connect request.
T_DATA	User data has arrived at the transport endpoint.
T_EXDATA	Expedited user data has arrived at the transport endpoint. (Expedited data will be discussed later in this chapter.)
T_DISCONNECT	A notification that the connection was aborted or that the server rejected a connect request, called a disconnect indication, has arrived at the transport endpoint.

T_ORDREL   A request for the orderly release of a connection,
                  called an orderly release indication, has arrived at the
                  transport endpoint.

T_UDERR   The notification of an error in a previously sent
                  datagram, called a unitdata error indication, has
                  arrived at the transport endpoint (see Chapter 4).

As described in the state tables of Appendix A, it is possible in some
states to receive one of several asynchronous events. The **t_look** [see
t_look(3N)] routine enables a user to determine what event has occurred if a
TLOOK error is returned. The user can then process that event accordingly.
In the example, if a connect request is rejected, the event passed to the client
will be a disconnect indication. The client will exit if its request is rejected.

The Server

Returning to the example, when the client calls **t_connect**, a connect indication will be generated on the server's listening transport endpoint. The
steps required by the server to process the event are presented below. For
each client, the server accepts the connect request and spawns a server process
to manage the connection.

```
    if ((call = (struct t_call *)t_alloc(listen_fd, T_CALL, T_ALL)) == NULL) {
        t_error("t_alloc of t_call structure failed");
        exit(5);
    }
    while (1) {
        if (t_listen(listen_fd, call) < 0) {
            t_error("t_listen failed for listen_fd");
            exit(6);
        }

        if ((conn_fd = accept_call(listen_fd, call)) != DISCONNECT)
            run_server(listen_fd);
    }
}
```

The server will loop forever, processing each connect indication. First, the server calls **t_listen** to retrieve the next connect indication. When one arrives, the server calls **accept_call** to accept the connect request. **accept_call** accepts the connection on an alternate transport endpoint (as discussed below) and returns the value of that endpoint. *conn_fd* is a global variable that identifies the transport endpoint where the connection is established. Because the connection is accepted on an alternate endpoint, the server may continue listening for connect indications on the endpoint that was bound for listening. If the call is accepted without error, **run_server** will spawn a process to manage the connection.

The server allocates a **t_call** structure to be used by **t_listen**. The third argument to **t_alloc**, T_ALL, specifies that all necessary buffers should be allocated for retrieving the caller's address, options, and user data. As mentioned earlier, the transport provider in this example does not support the transfer of user data during connection establishment, and also does not support any protocol options. Therefore, **t_alloc** will not allocate buffers for the user data and options. It must, however, allocate a buffer large enough to store the address of the caller. **t_alloc** determines the buffer size from the *addr* characteristic returned by **t_open**. The *maxlen* field of each **netbuf** structure will be set to the size of the newly allocated buffer by **t_alloc**. (*maxlen* is 0 for the user data and options buffers.)

Using the **t_call** structure, the server calls **t_listen** to retrieve the next connect indication. If one is currently available, it is returned to the server immediately. Otherwise, **t_listen** will block until a connect indication arrives.

 The Transport Interface supports an asynchronous mode for such routines that will prevent a process from blocking. This feature is discussed in Chapter 6.

When a connect indication arrives, the server calls **accept_call** to accept the client's request, as follows:

```
accept_call(listen_fd, call)
int listen_fd;
struct t_call *call;
{
   int resfd;

   if ((resfd = t_open("/dev/tivc", O_RDWR, NULL)) < 0) {
       t_error("t_open for responding fd failed");
       exit(7);
   }

   if (t_bind(resfd, NULL, NULL) < 0) {
       t_error("t_bind for responding fd failed");
       exit(8);
   }

   if (t_accept(listen_fd, resfd, call) < 0) {
       if (t_errno == TLOOK) {   /* must be a disconnect */
           if (t_rcvdis(listen_fd, NULL) < 0) {
               t_error("t_rcvdis failed for listen_fd");
               exit(9);
           }
           if (t_close(resfd) < 0) {
               t_error("t_close failed for responding fd");
               exit(10);
           }
           /* go back up and listen for other calls */
           return(DISCONNECT);
       }
       t_error("t_accept failed");
       exit(11);
   }
   return(resfd);
}
```

accept_call takes two arguments. *listen_fd* identifies the transport endpoint
where the connect indication arrived, and *call* is a pointer to a **t_call** structure
that contains all information associated with the connect indication. The
server will first establish another transport endpoint by opening the clone
device node of the transport provider and binding an address. As with the
client, a NULL value is passed to **t_bind** to specify that the user does not care

what address is bound by the provider. The newly established transport end-point, *resfd*, is used to accept the client's connect request.

The first two arguments of **t_accept** specify the listening transport end-point and the endpoint where the connection will be accepted, respectively. A connection may be accepted on the listening endpoint. However, this would prevent other clients from accessing the server for the duration of that connection.

The third argument of **t_accept** points to the **t_call** structure associated with the connect indication. This structure should contain the address of the calling user and the sequence number returned by **t_listen**. The value of *sequence* has particular significance if the server manages multiple outstanding connect indications. Chapter 6 presents such an example. Also, the **t_call** structure should identify protocol options the user would like to specify and user data that may be passed to the client. Because the transport provider in this example does not support protocol options or the transfer of user data during connection establishment, the **t_call** structure returned by **t_listen** may be passed without change to **t_accept**.

For simplicity in the example, the server will exit if either the **t_open** or **t_bind** call fails. **exit**(2) will close the transport endpoint associated with *listen_fd*, causing the transport provider to pass a disconnect indication to the client that requested the connection. This disconnect indication notifies the client that the connection was not established; **t_connect** will fail, setting **t_errno** to TLOOK.

t_accept may fail if an asynchronous event has occurred on the listening transport endpoint before the connection is accepted, and **t_errno** will be set to TLOOK. The state transition table in Appendix A shows that the only event that may occur in this state with only one outstanding connect indication is a disconnect indication. This event may occur if the client decides to undo the connect request it had previously initiated. If a disconnect indication arrives, the server must retrieve the disconnect indication using **t_rcvdis**. This routine takes a pointer to a **t_discon** structure as an argument, which is used to retrieve information associated with a disconnect indication. In this example, however, the server does not care to retrieve this information, so it sets the argument to NULL. After receiving the disconnect indication, **accept_call** closes the responding transport endpoint and returns DISCON-NECT, which informs the server that the connection was disconnected by the client. The server then listens for further connect indications.

Figure 3-1 illustrates how the server establishes connections.

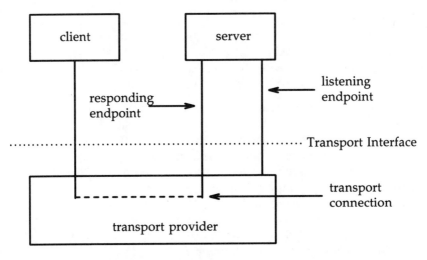

Figure 3-1: Listening and Responding Transport Endpoints

The transport connection is established on the newly created responding end-point, and the listening endpoint is freed to retrieve further connect indications.

Data Transfer

Once the connection has been established, both the client and server may begin transferring data over the connection using **t_snd** and **t_rcv**. In fact, the Transport Interface does not differentiate the client from the server from this point on. Either user may send and receive data, or release the connection. The Transport Interface guarantees reliable, sequenced delivery of data over an existing connection.

Two classes of data may be transferred over a transport connection: normal and expedited. Expedited data is typically associated with information of an urgent nature. The exact semantics of expedited data are subject to the interpretations of the transport provider. Furthermore, all transport protocols do not support the notion of an expedited data class [see *t_open*(3N)].

All transport protocols support the transfer of data in byte stream mode, where "byte stream" implies no concept of message boundaries on data that is transferred over a connection. However, some transport protocols support the preservation of message boundaries over a transport connection. This service is supported by the Transport Interface, but protocol-independent software must not rely on its existence.

The message interface for data transfer is supported by a special flag of **t_snd** and **t_rcv** called T_MORE. The messages, called Transport Service Data Units (TSDU), may be transferred between two transport users as distinct units. The maximum size of a TSDU is a characteristic of the underlying transport protocol. This information is available to the user from **t_open** and **t_getinfo**. Because the maximum TSDU size can be large (possibly unlimited), the Transport Interface enables a user to transmit a message in multiple units.

To send a message in multiple units over a transport connection, the user must set the T_MORE flag on every **t_snd** call except the last. This flag indicates that the user will send more data associated with the message in a subsequent call to **t_snd**. The last message unit should be transmitted with T_MORE turned off to indicate that this is the end of the TSDU.

Similarly, a TSDU may be passed to the user on the receiving side in multiple units. Again, if **t_rcv** returns with the T_MORE flag set, the user should continue calling **t_rcv** to retrieve the remainder of the message. The last unit in the message will be indicated by a call to **t_rcv** that does not set T_MORE.

The T_MORE flag implies nothing about how the data may be packaged below the Transport Interface. Furthermore, it implies nothing about how the data may be delivered to the remote user. Each transport protocol, and each implementation of that protocol, may package and deliver the data differently.

For example, if a user sends a complete message in a single call to **t_snd**, there is no guarantee that the transport provider will deliver the data in a single unit to the remote transport user. Similarly, a TSDU transmitted in two message units may be delivered in a single unit to the remote transport user. The message boundaries may only be preserved by noting the value of the T_MORE flag on **t_snd** and **t_rcv**. This will guarantee that the receiving user will see a message with the same contents and message boundaries as was sent by the remote user.

The Client

Continuing with the client/server example, the server will transfer a log file to the client over the transport connection. The client receives this data and writes it to its standard output file. A byte stream interface is used by the client and server, where message boundaries (that is, the T_MORE flag) are ignored. The client receives data using the following instructions:

```
while ((nbytes = t_rcv(fd, buf, 1024, &flags)) != -1) {
    if (fwrite(buf, 1, nbytes, stdout) < 0) {
        fprintf(stderr, "fwrite failed0);
        exit(5);
    }
}
```

The client continuously calls **t_rcv** to process incoming data. If no data is currently available, **t_rcv** blocks until data arrives. **t_rcv** will retrieve the available data up to 1024 bytes, which is the size of the client's input buffer, and will return the number of bytes that were received. The client then writes this data to standard output and continues. The data transfer phase will complete when **t_rcv** fails. **t_rcv** will fail if an orderly release indication or disconnect indication arrives, as will be discussed later in this chapter. If the **fwrite** call [see *fwrite*(3S)] fails for any reason, the client will exit, thereby closing the transport endpoint. If the transport endpoint is closed (either by **exit** or **t_close**) when it is in the data transfer phase, the connection will be aborted and the remote user will receive a disconnect indication.

The Server

Looking now at the other side of the connection, the server manages its data transfer by spawning a child process to send the data to the client. The parent process then loops back to listen for further connect indications. **run_server** is called by the server to spawn this child process as follows:

```
connrelease( )
{
    /* conn_fd is global because needed here */
    if (t_look(conn_fd) == T_DISCONNECT) {
        fprintf(stderr, "connection aborted0);
        exit(12);
    }
    /* else orderly release indication - normal exit */
    exit(0);
}
run_server(listen_fd)
int listen_fd;
{
    int nbytes;
    FILE *logfp;        /* file pointer to log file */
    char buf[1024];

    switch (fork( )) {

    case -1:
        perror("fork failed");
        exit(20);

    default:    /* parent */

        /* close conn_fd and then go up and listen again */
        if (t_close(conn_fd) < 0) {
            t_error("t_close failed for conn_fd");
            exit(21);
        }
```

continued

```
    return;

case 0:     /* child */

    /* close listen_fd and do service */
    if (t_close(listen_fd) < 0) {
        t_error("t_close failed for listen_fd");
        exit(22);
    }
    if ((logfp = fopen("logfile", "r")) == NULL) {
        perror("cannot open logfile");
        exit(23);
    }

    signal(SIGPOLL, connrelease);
    if (ioctl(conn_fd, I_SETSIG, S_INPUT) < 0) {
        perror("ioctl I_SETSIG failed");
        exit(24);
    }
    if (t_look(conn_fd) != 0) { /* was disconnect already there? */
        fprintf(stderr, "t_look returned unexpected event0);
        exit(25);
    }

    while ((nbytes = fread(buf, 1, 1024, logfp)) > 0)
        if (t_snd(conn_fd, buf, nbytes, 0) < 0) {
            t_error("t_snd failed");
            exit(26);
        }
```

After the **fork**, the parent process will return to the main processing loop and listen for further connect indications. Meanwhile, the child process will manage the newly established transport connection. If the **fork** call fails, **exit** will close the transport endpoint associated with *listen_fd*. This action will cause a disconnect indication to be passed to the client, and the client's **t_connect** call will fail.

The server process reads 1024 bytes of the log file at a time and sends that data to the client using **t_snd**. *buf* points to the start of the data buffer, and *nbytes* specifies the number of bytes to be transmitted. The fourth argument is used to specify optional flags. Two flags are currently supported: T_EXPEDITED may be set to indicate that the data is expedited, and T_MORE may be set to define message boundaries when transmitting messages over a connection. Neither flag is set by the server in this example.

If the user begins to flood the transport provider with data, the provider may exert back pressure to provide flow control. In such cases, **t_snd** will block until the flow control is relieved, and will then resume its operation. **t_snd** will not complete until *nbyte* bytes have been passed to the transport provider.

The **t_snd** routine does not look for a disconnect indication (signifying that the connection was broken) before passing data to the provider. Also, because the data traffic is flowing in one direction, the user will never look for incoming events. If, for some reason, the connection is aborted, the user should be notified because data may be lost. One option available to the user is to use **t_look** to check for incoming events before each **t_snd** call. A more efficient solution is the one presented in the example. The STREAMS I_SETSIG **ioctl** enables a user to request a signal when a given event occurs [see *streamio*(7) and *signal*(2)]. The STREAMS event of concern here is S_INPUT, which will cause a signal to be sent to the user if any input arrives on the Stream referenced by *conn_fd*. If a disconnect indication arrives, the signal catching routine (**connrelease**) will print an appropriate error message and then exit.

If the data traffic flowed in both directions in this example, the user would not have to monitor the connection for disconnects. If the client alternated **t_snd** and **t_rcv** calls, it could rely on **t_rcv** to recognize an incoming disconnect indication.

Connection Release

At any point during data transfer, either user may release the transport connection and end the conversation. As mentioned earlier, two forms of connection release are supported by the Transport Interface. The first, abortive release, breaks a connection immediately and may result in the loss of any data that has not yet reached the destination user. **t_snddis** may be called by either user to generate an abortive release. Also, the transport provider may abort a connection if a problem occurs below the Transport Interface. **t_snddis** enables a user to send data to the remote user when aborting a connection. Although the abortive release is supported by all transport providers, the ability to send data when aborting a connection is not.

When the remote user is notified of the aborted connection, **t_rcvdis** must be called to retrieve the disconnect indication. This call will return a reason code that indicates why the connection was aborted, and will return any user data that may have accompanied the disconnect indication (if the abortive release was initiated by the remote user). This reason code is specific to the underlying transport protocol, and should not be interpreted by protocol-independent software.

The second form of connection release is orderly release, which gracefully terminates a connection and guarantees that no data will be lost. All transport providers must support the abortive release procedure, but orderly release is an optional facility that is not supported by all transport protocols.

The Server

The client/server example in this chapter assumes that the transport provider does support the orderly release of a connection. When all the data has been transferred by the server, the connection may be released as follows:

```
        if (t_sndrel(conn_fd) < 0) {
            t_error("t_sndrel failed");
            exit(27);
        }
        pause( );    /* until orderly release indication arrives */
    }
}
```

The orderly release procedure consists of two steps by each user. The first user to complete data transfer may initiate a release using **t_sndrel**, as illustrated in the example. This routine informs the client that no more data will be sent by the server. When the client receives such an indication, it may continue sending data back to the server if desired. When all data has been transferred, however, the client must also call **t_sndrel** to indicate that it is ready to release the connection. The connection will be released only after both users have requested an orderly release and received the corresponding indication from the other user.

In this example, data is transferred in one direction from the server to the client, so the server does not expect to receive data from the client after it has initiated the release procedure. Thus, the server simply calls **pause** [see *pause*(2)] after initiating the release. Eventually, the remote user will respond with its orderly release request, and the indication will generate a signal that will be caught by **connrelease**. Remember that the server earlier issued an I_SETSIG **ioctl** call to generate a signal on any incoming event. Since the only possible Transport Interface events that can occur in this situation are a disconnect indication or orderly release indication, **connrelease** will terminate normally when the orderly release indication arrives. The **exit** call in **connrelease** will close the transport endpoint, thereby freeing the bound address for use by another user. If a user process wants to close a transport endpoint without exiting, it may call **t_close**.

The Client

The client's view of connection release is similar to that of the server. As mentioned earlier, the client continues to process incoming data until **t_rcv** fails. If the server releases the connection (using either **t_snddis** or **t_sndrel**), **t_rcv** will fail and set **t_errno** to TLOOK. The client then processes the connection release as follows:

```
if ((t_errno == TLOOK)  &&  (t_look(fd) == T_ORDREL)) {
    if (t_rcvrel(fd) < 0) {
        t_error("t_rcvrel failed");
        exit(6);
    }
    if (t_sndrel(fd) < 0) {
        t_error("t_sndrel failed");
        exit(7);
    }
    exit(0);
}
t_error("t_rcv failed");
exit(8);
}
```

Under normal circumstances, the client terminates the transfer of data by calling **t_sndrel** to initiate the connection release. When the orderly release indication arrives at the client's side of the connection, the client checks to make sure the expected orderly release indication has arrived. If so, it proceeds with the release procedures by calling **t_rcvrel** to process the indication and **t_sndrel** to inform the server that it is also ready to release the connection. At this point the client exits, thereby closing its transport endpoint.

Because all transport providers do not support the orderly release facility just described, users may have to use the abortive release facility provided by **t_snddis** and **t_rcvdis**. However, steps must be taken by each user to prevent any loss of data. For example, a special byte pattern may be inserted in the data stream to indicate the end of a conversation. Many mechanisms are possible for preventing data loss. Each application and high-level protocol must choose an appropriate mechanism given the target protocol environment and requirements.

4 Connectionless-mode Service

Introduction

This chapter describes the connectionless-mode service of the Transport Interface. Connectionless-mode service is appropriate for short-term request/response interactions, such as transaction processing applications. Data are transferred in self-contained units with no logical relationship required among multiple units.

The connectionless-mode services will be described using a transaction server as an example. This server waits for incoming transaction queries, and processes and responds to each query.

Local Management

Just as with connection-mode service, the transport users must perform appropriate local management steps before data can be transferred. A user must choose the appropriate connectionless service provider using **t_open** and establish its identity using **t_bind**.

t_optmgmt may be used to negotiate protocol options that may be associated with the transfer of each data unit. As with the connection-mode service, each transport provider specifies the options, if any, that it supports. Option negotiation is therefore a protocol-specific activity.

In the example, the definitions and local management calls needed by the transaction server are as follows:

```
#include <stdio.h>
#include <fcntl.h>
#include <tiuser.h>


#define SRV_ADDR    2       /* server's well-known address */


main( )
{
   int fd;
   int flags;

   struct t_bind *bind;
   struct t_unitdata *ud;
   struct t_uderr *uderr;

   extern int t_errno;

   if ((fd = t_open("/dev/tidg", O_RDWR, NULL)) < 0) {
       t_error("unable to open /dev/provider");
       exit(1);
   }
```

continued

```
if ((bind = (struct t_bind *)t_alloc(fd, T_BIND, T_ADDR)) == NULL) {
    t_error("t_alloc of t_bind structure failed");
    exit(2);
}


bind->addr.len = sizeof(int);
*(int *)bind->addr.buf = SRV_ADDR;
bind->qlen = 0;


if (t_bind(fd, bind, bind) < 0) {
    t_error("t_bind failed");
    exit(3);
}


/*
 * is the bound address correct?
 */


if (*(int *)bind->addr.buf != SRV_ADDR) {
    fprintf(stderr, "t_bind bound wrong address0);
    exit(4);
}
```

The local management steps should look familiar by now. The server establishes a transport endpoint with the desired transport provider using **t_open**. Each provider has an associated service type, so the user may choose a particular service by opening the appropriate transport provider file. This connectionless-mode server ignores the characteristics of the provider returned by **t_open** in the same way as the users in the connection-mode example, setting the third argument to NULL. For simplicity, the transaction server assumes the transport provider has the following characteristics:

■ The transport address is an integer value that uniquely identifies each user.

■ The transport provider supports the T_CLTS service type (connection-less transport service, or datagram).

■ The transport provider does not support any protocol-specific options.

The connectionless server also binds a transport address to the endpoint so that potential clients may identify and access the server. A **t_bind** structure is allocated using **t_alloc**, and the *buf* and *len* fields of the address are set accordingly.

One important difference between the connection-mode server and this connectionless-mode server is that the *qlen* field of the **t_bind** structure has no meaning for connectionless-mode service. That is because all users are capable of receiving datagrams once they have bound an address. The Transport Interface defines an inherent client/server relationship between two users while establishing a transport connection in the connection-mode service. However, no such relationship exists in the connectionless-mode service. It is the context of this example, not the Transport Interface, that defines one user as a server and another as a client.

Because the address of the server is known by all potential clients, the server checks the bound address returned by **t_bind** to ensure it is correct.

Data Transfer

Once a user has bound an address to the transport endpoint, datagrams may be sent or received over that endpoint. Each outgoing message is accompanied by the address of the destination user. In addition, the Transport Interface enables a user to specify protocol options that should be associated with the transfer of the data unit (for example, transit delay). As discussed earlier, each transport provider defines the set of options, if any, that may accompany a datagram. When the datagram is passed to the destination user, the associated protocol options may be returned as well.

The following sequence of calls illustrates the data transfer phase of the connectionless-mode server:

```
if ((ud = (struct t_unitdata *)t_alloc(fd, T_UNITDATA, T_ALL)) == NULL) {
    t_error("t_alloc of t_unitdata structure failed");
    exit(5);
}

if ((uderr = (struct t_uderr *)t_alloc(fd, T_UDERROR, T_ALL)) == NULL) {
    t_error("t_alloc of t_uderr structure failed");
    exit(6);
}

while (1) {
    if (t_rcvudata(fd, ud, &flags) < 0) {
        if (t_errno == TLOOK) {

            /*
             * Error on previously sent datagram
             */

            if (t_rcvuderr(fd, uderr) < 0) {
                exit(7);
            }

            fprintf(stderr, "bad datagram, error = %d0,
                uderr->error);
            continue;
        }
```

continued

```
            t_error("t_rcvudata failed");
            exit(8);
        }

        /*
         * Query( ) processes the request and places the
         * response in ud->udata.buf, setting ud->udata.len
         */

        query(ud);

        if (t_sndudata(fd, ud, 0) < 0) {
            t_error("t_sndudata failed");
            exit(9);
        }
    }
}

query( )
{

    /* Merely a stub for simplicity */

}
```

The server must first allocate a **t_unitdata** structure for storing datagrams, which has the following format:

```
struct t_unitdata {
    struct netbuf addr;
    struct netbuf opt;
    struct netbuf udata;
}
```

addr holds the source address of incoming datagrams and the destination address of outgoing datagrams, *opt* identifies any protocol options associated with the transfer of the datagram, and *udata* holds the data itself. The *addr*, *opt*, and *udata* fields must all be allocated with buffers that are large enough to hold any possible incoming values. As described in the previous chapter, the T_ALL argument to **t_alloc** will ensure this and will set the *maxlen* field of each **netbuf** structure accordingly. Because the provider does not support protocol options in this example, no options buffer will be allocated, and *maxlen* will be set to zero in the **netbuf** structure for options. A **t_uderr** structure is also allocated by the server for processing any datagram errors, as will be discussed later in this chapter.

The transaction server loops forever, receiving queries, processing the queries, and responding to the clients. It first calls **t_rcvudata** to receive the next query. **t_rcvudata** will retrieve the next available incoming datagram. If none is currently available, **t_rcvudata** will block, waiting for a datagram to arrive. The second argument of **t_rcvudata** identifies the **t_unitdata** structure where the datagram should be stored.

The third argument, *flags*, must point to an integer variable and may be set to T_MORE on return from **t_rcvudata** to indicate that the user's *udata* buffer was not large enough to store the full datagram. In this case, subsequent calls to **t_rcvudata** will retrieve the remainder of the datagram. Because **t_alloc** allocates a *udata* buffer large enough to store the maximum datagram size, the transaction server does not have to check the value of *flags*.

If a datagram is received successfully, the transaction server calls the *query* routine to process the request. This routine will store the response in the structure pointed to by *ud*, and will set *ud->udata.len* to indicate the number of bytes in the response. The source address returned by **t_rcvudata** in *ud->addr* will be used as the destination address by **t_sndudata**.

When the response is ready, **t_sndudata** is called to return the response to the client. The Transport Interface prevents a user from flooding the transport provider with datagrams using the same flow control mechanism described for the connection-mode service. In such cases, **t_sndudata** will block until the flow control is relieved, and will then resume its operation.

Datagram Errors

If the transport provider cannot process a datagram that was passed to it by **t_sndudata**, it will return a unit data error event, T_UDERR, to the user. This event includes the destination address and options associated with the datagram, plus a protocol-specific error value that describes what may be wrong with the datagram. The reason a datagram could not be processed is protocol-specific. One reason may be that the transport provider could not interpret the destination address or options. Each transport protocol is expected to specify all reasons for which it is unable to process a datagram.

 NOTE The unit data error indication is not necessarily intended to indicate success or failure in delivering the datagram to the specified destination. The transport protocol decides how the indication will be used. Remember, the connectionless service does not guarantee reliable delivery of data.

The transaction server will be notified of this error event when it attempts to receive another datagram. In this case, **t_rcvudata** will fail, setting **t_errno** to TLOOK. If TLOOK is set, the only possible event is T_UDERR, so the server calls **t_rcvuderr** to retrieve the event. The second argument to **t_rcvuderr** is the **t_uderr** structure that was allocated earlier. This structure is filled in by **t_rcvuderr** and has the following format:

```
struct t_uderr {
    struct netbuf addr;
    struct netbuf opt;
    long error;
}
```

where *addr* and *opt* identify the destination address and protocol options as specified in the bad datagram, and *error* is a protocol-specific error code that indicates why the provider could not process the datagram. The transaction server prints the error code and then continues by entering the processing loop again.

5 A Read/Write Interface

Introduction

A user may wish to establish a transport connection and then **exec** [see *exec*(2)] an existing user program such as **cat** [see *cat*(1)] to process the data as it arrives over the connection. However, existing programs use **read** and **write** for their I/O needs. The Transport Interface does not directly support a **read/write** interface to a transport provider, but one is available with UNIX System V/386. This interface enables a user to issue **read** and **write** calls over a transport connection that is in the data transfer phase. This chapter describes the **read/write** interface to the connection-mode service of the Transport Interface. This interface is not available with the connectionless-mode service.

The **read/write** interface is presented using the client example of Chapter 3 with some minor modifications. The clients are identical until the data transfer phase is reached. At that point, this client will use the **read/write** interface and **cat** to process incoming data. **cat** can be run without change over the transport connection. Only the differences between this client and that of the example in Chapter 3 are shown below.

```
#include <stropts.h>
    .
    .    /*
    .     * Same local management and connection
    .     * establishment steps.
    .     */
    .
    if (ioctl(fd, I_PUSH, "tirdwr") < 0) {
        perror("I_PUSH of tirdwr failed");
        exit(5);
    }

    close(0);
    dup(fd);
    execl("/bin/cat", "/bin/cat", 0);
    perror("execl of /bin/cat failed");
    exit(6);
}
```

The client invokes the **read/write** interface by pushing the **tirdwr** [see *tirdwr*(7)] module onto the Stream associated with the transport endpoint where the connection was established [see L_PUSH in *streamio*(7)]. This module converts the Transport Interface above the transport provider into a pure **read/write** interface. With the module in place, the client calls **close** [see *close*(2)] and **dup** [see *dup*(2)] to establish the transport endpoint as its standard input file, and uses **/bin/cat** to process the input. Because the transport endpoint identifier is a file descriptor, the facility for **dup**ing the endpoint is available to users.

Because the Transport Interface has been implemented using STREAMS, the facilities of this character I/O mechanism can be used to provide enhanced user services. By pushing the **tirdwr** module above the transport provider, the user's interface is effectively changed. The semantics of **read** and **write** must be followed, and message boundaries will not be preserved.

 The **tirdwr** module may only be pushed onto a Stream when the transport endpoint is in the data transfer phase. Once the module is pushed, the user may not call any Transport Interface routines. If a Transport Interface routine is invoked, **tirdwr** will generate a fatal protocol error, EPROTO, on that Stream, rendering it unusable. Furthermore, if the user pops the **tirdwr** module off the Stream [see L_POP in *streamio*(7)], the transport connection will be aborted.

The exact semantics of **write**, **read**, and **close** using **tirdwr** are described below. To summarize, **tirdwr** enables a user to send and receive data over a transport connection using **read** and **write**. This module will translate all Transport Interface indications into the appropriate actions. The connection can be released with the **close** system call.

write

The user may transmit data over the transport connection using **write**. The **tirdwr** module will pass data through to the transport provider. However, if a user attempts to send a zero-length data packet, which the STREAMS mechanism allows, **tirdwr** will discard the message. If for some reason the transport connection is aborted (for example the remote user aborts the connection using **t_snddis**), a STREAMS hangup condition will be generated on that Stream, and further **write** calls will fail and set *errno* to ENXIO. The user can still retrieve any available data after a hangup, however.

read

read may be used to retrieve data that has arrived over the transport connection. The **tirdwr** module will pass data through to the user from the transport provider. However, any other event or indication passed to the user from the provider will be processed by **tirdwr** as follows:

- **read** cannot process expedited data because it cannot distinguish expedited data from normal data for the user. If an expedited data indication is received, **tirdwr** will generate a fatal protocol error, EPROTO, on that Stream. This error will cause further system calls to fail. You must therefore be aware that you should not communicate with a process that is sending expedited data.

- If an abortive disconnect indication is received, **tirdwr** will discard the indication and generate a STREAMS hangup condition on that Stream. Subsequent **read** calls will retrieve any remaining data, and then **read** will return zero for all further calls (indicating end-of-file).

- If an orderly release indication is received, **tirdwr** will discard the indication and deliver a zero-length STREAMS message to the user. As described in **read**, this notifies the user of end-of-file by returning 0 to the user.

- If any other Transport Interface indication is received, **tirdwr** will generate a fatal protocol error, EPROTO, on that Stream. This will cause further system calls to fail. If a user pushes **tirdwr** onto a Stream after the connection has been established, such indications will not be generated.

Close

With **tirdwr** on a Stream, the user can send and receive data over a transport connection for the duration of that connection. Either user may terminate the connection by closing the file descriptor associated with the transport endpoint or by popping the **tirdwr** module off the Stream. In either case, **tirdwr** will take the following actions:

■ If an orderly release indication had previously been received by **tirdwr**, an orderly release request will be passed to the transport provider to complete the orderly release of the connection. The remote user, who initiated the orderly release procedure, will receive the expected indication when data transfer completes.

■ If a disconnect indication had previously been received by **tirdwr**, no special action is taken.

■ If neither an orderly release indication nor disconnect indication had previously been received by **tirdwr**, a disconnect request will be passed to the transport provider to abortively release the connection.

■ If an error had previously occurred on the Stream and a disconnect indication has not been received by **tirdwr**, a disconnect request will be passed to the transport provider.

A process may not initiate an orderly release after **tirdwr** is pushed onto a Stream, but **tirdwr** will handle an orderly release properly if it is initiated by the user on the other side of a transport connection. If the client in this chapter is communicating with the server program in Chapter 3, that server will terminate the transfer of data with an orderly release request. The server then waits for the corresponding indication from the client. At that point, the client exits and the transport endpoint is closed. As explained in the first bullet item above, when the file descriptor is closed, **tirdwr** will initiate the orderly release request from the client's side of the connection. This will generate the indication that the server is expecting, and the connection will be released properly.

6 Advanced Topics

Introduction

This chapter presents important concepts of the Transport Interface that have not been covered in the previous chapters. First, an optional non-blocking (asynchronous) mode for some library calls is described. Then, an advanced programming example is presented that defines a server that supports multiple outstanding connect indications and operates in an event-driven manner.

Asynchronous Execution Mode

Many Transport Interface library routines may block waiting for an incoming event or the relaxation of flow control. However, some time-critical applications should not block for any reason. Similarly, an application may wish to do local processing while waiting for some asynchronous Transport Interface event.

Support for asynchronous processing of Transport Interface events is available to applications using a combination of the STREAMS asynchronous features and the non-blocking mode of the Transport Interface library routines. Earlier examples in this guide have illustrated the use of the STREAMS **poll** system call and the I_SETSIG **ioctl** command for processing events in an asynchronous manner.

In addition, each Transport Interface routine that may block waiting for some event can be run in a special non-blocking mode. For example, **t_listen** will normally block, waiting for a connect indication. However, a server can periodically poll a transport endpoint for existing connect indications by calling **t_listen** in the non-blocking (or asynchronous) mode. The asynchronous mode is enabled by setting O_NDELAY on the file descriptor. This can be set as a flag on **t_open**, or by calling **fcntl** [see *fcntl*(2)] before calling the Transport Interface routine. **fcntl** can be used to enable or disable this mode at any time. All programming examples illustrated throughout this guide use the default, synchronous mode of processing.

O_NDELAY affects each Transport Interface routine in a different manner. To determine the exact semantics of O_NDELAY for a particular routine, see the appropriate pages in Section 3N of the *Programmer's Reference Manual*.

Advanced Programming Example

The following example demonstrates two important concepts. The first is a server's ability to manage multiple outstanding connect indications. The second is an illustration of the ability to write event-driven software using the Transport Interface and the STREAMS system call interface.

The server example in Chapter 3 is capable of supporting only one outstanding connect indication, but the Transport Interface supports the ability to manage multiple outstanding connect indications. One reason a server might wish to receive several, simultaneous connect indications is to impose a priority scheme on each client. A server may retrieve several connect indications, and then accept them in an order based on a priority associated with each client. A second reason for handling several outstanding connect indications is that the single-threaded scheme has some limitations. Depending on the implementation of the transport provider, it is possible that while the server is processing the current connect indication, other clients will find it busy. If, however, multiple connect indications can be processed simultaneously, the server will be found to be busy only if the maximum allowed number of clients attempt to call the server simultaneously.

The server example is event-driven: the process polls a transport endpoint for incoming Transport Interface events and then takes the appropriate actions for the current event. The example demonstrates the ability to poll multiple transport endpoints for incoming events.

The definitions and local management functions needed by this example are similar to those of the server example in Chapter 3.

```
#include <tiuser.h>
#include <fcntl.h>
#include <stdio.h>
#include <poll.h>
#include <stropts.h>
#include <signal.h>


#define NUM_FDS          1
#define MAX_CONN_IND     4
#define SRV_ADDR         1        /* server's well-known address */


int conn_fd;                          /* server connection here */
struct t_call *calls[NUM_FDS][MAX_CONN_IND];/* holds connect indications */
extern int t_errno;

main( )
{
    struct pollfd pollfds[NUM_FDS];
    struct t_bind *bind;
    int i;

    /*
     * Only opening and binding one transport endpoint,
     * but more could be supported
     */
    if ((pollfds[0].fd = t_open("/dev/tivc", O_RDWR, NULL)) < 0) {
        t_error("t_open failed");
        exit(1);
    }

    if ((bind = (struct t_bind *)t_alloc(pollfds[0].fd, T_BIND, T_ALL)) == NULL) {
        t_error("t_alloc of t_bind structure failed");
        exit(2);
    }
    bind->qlen = MAX_CONN_IND;
    bind->addr.len = sizeof(int);
    *(int *)bind->addr.buf = SRV_ADDR;
```

```
                                                             continued

    if (t_bind(pollfds[0].fd, bind, bind) < 0) {
        t_error("t_bind failed");
        exit(3);
    }


    /*
     * Was the correct address bound?
     */
    if (*(int *)bind->addr.buf != SRV_ADDR) {
        fprintf(stderr, "t_bind bound wrong address0);
        exit(4);
    }
```

The file descriptor returned by **t_open** is stored in a **pollfd** structure [see *poll*(2)] that will be used to poll the transport endpoint for incoming data. Notice that only one transport endpoint is established in this example. However, the remainder of the example is written to manage multiple transport endpoints. Several endpoints could be supported with minor changes to the above code.

An important aspect of this server is that it sets *qlen* to a value greater than 1 for **t_bind**. This indicates that the server is willing to handle multiple outstanding connect indications. Remember that the earlier examples single-threaded the connect indications and responses. The server would accept the current connect indication before retrieving additional connect indications. This example, however, can retrieve up to MAX_CONN_IND connect indications at one time before responding to any of them. The transport provider may negotiate the value of *qlen* downward if it cannot support MAX_CONN_IND outstanding connect indications.

Once the server has bound its address and is ready to process incoming connect requests, it does the following:

```
pollfds[0].events = POLLIN;
while (1) {
    if (poll(pollfds, NUM_FDS, -1) < 0) {
        perror("poll failed");
        exit(5);
    }

    for (i = 0; i < NUM_FDS; i++) {

        switch (pollfds[i].revents) {

        default:
            perror("poll returned error event");
            exit(6);

        case 0:
            continue;

        case POLLIN:
            do_event(i, pollfds[i].fd);
            service_conn_ind(i, pollfds[i].fd);
        }
    }
}
```

The *events* field of the **pollfd** structure is set to POLLIN, which will notify the server of any incoming Transport Interface events. The server then enters an infinite loop, in which it will **poll** the transport endpoint(s) for events, and then process those events as they occur.

The **poll** call will block indefinitely, waiting for an incoming event. On return, each entry (corresponding to each transport endpoint) is checked for an existing event. If *revents* is set to 0, no event has occurred on that endpoint. In this case, the server continues to the next transport endpoint. If *revents* is set to POLLIN, an event does exist on the endpoint. In this case, **do_event** is called to process the event. If *revents* contains any other value, an error must have occurred on the transport endpoint and the server will exit.

For each iteration of the loop, if any event is found on the transport end-point, **service_conn_ind** is called to process any outstanding connect indications. However, if another connect indication is pending, **service_conn_ind** will save the current connect indication and respond to it later. This routine will be explained shortly.

If an incoming event is discovered, the following routine is called to process it:

```
do_event(slot, fd)
{
  struct t_discon *discon;
  int i;

  switch (t_look(fd)) {

  default:
    fprintf(stderr,"t_look returned an unexpected evento);
    exit(7);

  case T_ERROR:
    fprintf(stderr,"t_look returned T_ERROR evento);
    exit(8);

  case -1:
    t_error("t_look failed");
    exit(9);

  case 0:
    /* since POLLIN returned, this should not happen */
    fprintf(stderr,"t_look returned no evento);
    exit(10);

  case T_LISTEN:
    /*
     * find free element in calls array
     */
    for (i = 0; i < MAX_CONN_IND; i++) {
      if (calls[slot][i] == NULL)
        break;
    }
    if ((calls[slot][i] = (struct t_call *)t_alloc(fd, T_CALL, T_ALL)) == NULL) {
      t_error("t_alloc of t_call structure failed");
      exit(11);
    }
    if (t_listen(fd, calls[slot][i]) < 0) {
      t_error("t_listen failed");
```

continued

```
        exit(12);
    }
    break;

case T_DISCONNECT:
    discon = (struct t_discon *)t_alloc(fd, T_DIS, T_ALL);

    if (t_rcvdis(fd, discon) < 0) {
        t_error("t_rcvdis failed");
        exit(13);
    }
    /*
     * find call ind in array and delete it
     */
    for (i = 0; i < MAX_CONN_IND; i++) {
        if (discon->sequence == calls[slot][i]->sequence) {
            t_free(calls[slot][i], T_CALL);
            calls[slot][i] = NULL;
        }
    }
    t_free(discon, T_DIS);
    break;
    }
}
```

This routine takes a number, *slot*, and a file descriptor, *fd*, as arguments. *slot* is used as an index into the global array *calls*. This array contains an entry for each polled transport endpoint, where each entry consists of an array of **t_call** structures that hold incoming connect indications for that transport endpoint. The value of *slot* is used to identify the transport endpoint of interest.

do_event calls **t_look** to determine the Transport Interface event that has occurred on the transport endpoint referenced by *fd*. If a connect indication (T_LISTEN event) or disconnect indication (T_DISCONNECT event) has arrived, the event is processed. Otherwise, the server prints an appropriate error message and exits.

For connect indications, **do_event** scans the array of outstanding connect indications looking for the first free entry. A **t_call** structure is then allocated for that entry, and the connect indication is retrieved using **t_listen**. There must always be at least one free entry in the connect indication array because the array is large enough to hold the maximum number of outstanding connect indications as negotiated by **t_bind**. The processing of the connect indication is deferred until later.

If a disconnect indication arrives, it must correspond to a previously received connect indication. This scenario arises if a client attempts to undo a previous connect request. In this case, **do_event** allocates a **t_discon** structure to retrieve the relevant disconnect information. This structure has the following members:

```
struct t_discon {
    struct netbuf udata;
    int reason;
    int sequence;
}
```

where *udata* identifies any user data that might have been sent with the disconnect indication, *reason* contains a protocol-specific disconnect reason code, and *sequence* identifies the outstanding connect indication that matches this disconnect indication.

Next, **t_rcvdis** is called to retrieve the disconnect indication. The array of connect indications for *slot* is then scanned for one that contains a sequence number that matches the *sequence* number in the disconnect indication. When the connect indication is found, it is freed and the corresponding entry is set to NULL.

As mentioned earlier, if any event is found on a transport endpoint, **service_conn_ind** is called to process all currently outstanding connect indications associated with that endpoint as follows:

```
service_conn_ind(slot, fd)
{
    int i;

    for (i = 0; i < MAX_CONN_IND; i++) {
        if (calls[slot][i] == NULL)
            continue;

        if ((conn_fd = t_open("/dev/tivc", O_RDWR, NULL)) < 0) {
            t_error("open failed");
            exit(14);
        }
        if (t_bind(conn_fd, NULL, NULL) < 0) {
            t_error("t_bind failed");
            exit(15);
        }

        if (t_accept(fd, conn_fd, calls[slot][i]) < 0) {
            if (t_errno == TLOOK) {
                t_close(conn_fd);
                return;
            }
            t_error("t_accept failed");
            exit(16);
        }
        t_free(calls[slot][i], T_CALL);
        calls[slot][i] = NULL;

        run_server(fd);
    }
}
```

For the given slot (the transport endpoint), the array of outstanding connect
indications is scanned. For each indication, the server will open a responding
transport endpoint, bind an address to the endpoint, and then accept the connection on that endpoint. If another event (connect indication or disconnect
indication) arrives before the current indication is accepted, **t_accept** will fail
and set **t_errno** to TLOOK.

NOTE   The user cannot accept an outstanding connect indication if any pending connect indication events or disconnect indication events exist on that transport endpoint.

If this error occurs, the responding transport endpoint is closed and **service_conn_ind** will return immediately (saving the current connect indication for later processing). This causes the server's main processing loop to be entered, and the new event will be discovered by the next call to **poll**. In this way, multiple connect indications may be queued by the user.

Eventually, all events will be processed, and **service_conn_ind** will be able to accept each connect indication in turn. Once the connection has been established, the **run_server** routine used by the server in Chapter 3 is called to manage the data transfer.

A   Appendix A: State Transitions

Appendix A: State Transitions

The tables in this appendix describe all state transitions associated with the Transport Interface. First, however, the states and events will be described.

Transport Interface States

Figure A-1 defines the states used to describe the Transport Interface state transitions.

State	Description	Service Type
T_UNINIT	uninitialized – initial and final state of interface	T_COTS, T_COTS_ORD, T_CLTS
T_UNBND	initialized but not bound	T_COTS, T_COTS_ORD, T_CLTS
T_IDLE	no connection established	T_COTS, T_COTS_ORD, T_CLTS
T_OUTCON	outgoing connection pending for client	T_COTS, T_COTS_ORD
T_INCON	incoming connection pending for server	T_COTS, T_COTS_ORD
T_DATAXFER	data transfer	T_COTS, T_COTS_ORD
T_OUTREL	outgoing orderly release (waiting for orderly release indication)	T_COTS_ORD
T_INREL	incoming orderly release (waiting to send orderly release request)	T_COTS_ORD

Figure A-1: Transport Interface States

Outgoing Events

The outgoing events described in Figure A-2 correspond to the return of the specified transport routines, where these routines send a request or response to the transport provider.

In the figure, some events (such as *acceptN*) are distinguished by the context in which they occur. The context is based on the values of the following variables:

ocnt   count of outstanding connect indications

fd   file descriptor of the current transport endpoint

resfd   file descriptor of the transport endpoint where a connection will be accepted

Event	Description	Service Type
opened	successful return of **t_open**	T_COTS, T_COTS_ORD, T_CLTS
bind	successful return of **t_bind**	T_COTS, T_COTS_ORD, T_CLTS
optmgmt	successful return of **t_optmgmt**	T_COTS, T_COTS_ORD, T_CLTS
unbind	successful return of **t_unbind**	T_COTS, T_COTS_ORD, T_CLTS
closed	successful return of **t_close**	T_COTS, T_COTS_ORD, T_CLTS
connect1	successful return of **t_connect** in synchronous mode	T_COTS, T_COTS_ORD
connect2	TNODATA error on **t_connect** in asynchronous mode, or TLOOK error due to a disconnect indication arriving on the transport endpoint	T_COTS, T_COTS_ORD
accept1	successful return of **t_accept** with *ocnt* == 1, *fd* == *resfd*	T_COTS, T_COTS_ORD
accept2	successful return of **t_accept** with *ocnt* == 1, *fd* != *resfd*	T_COTS, T_COTS_ORD
accept3	successful return of **t_accept** with *ocnt* > 1	T_COTS, T_COTS_ORD
snd	successful return of **t_snd**	T_COTS, T_COTS_ORD
snddis1	successful return of **t_snddis** with *ocnt* <= 1	T_COTS, T_COTS_ORD
snddis2	successful return of **t_snddis** with *ocnt* > 1	T_COTS, T_COTS_ORD
sndrel	successful return of **t_sndrel**	T_COTS_ORD
sndudata	successful return of **t_sndudata**	T_CLTS

Figure A-2: Transport Interface Outgoing Events

Incoming Events

The incoming events correspond to the successful return of the specified routines, where these routines retrieve data or event information from the transport provider. The only incoming event not associated directly with the return of a routine is *pass_conn*, which occurs when a user transfers a connection to another transport endpoint. This event occurs on the endpoint that is being passed the connection, despite the fact that no Transport Interface routine is issued on that endpoint. *pass_conn* is included in the state tables to describe the behavior when a user accepts a connection on another transport endpoint.

In Figure A-3, the *rcvdis* events are distinguished by the context in which they occur. The context is based on the value of *ocnt*, which is the count of outstanding connect indications on the transport endpoint.

Incoming Event	Description	Service Type
listen	successful return of **t_listen**	T_COTS, T_COTS_ORD
rcvconnect	successful return of **t_rcvconnect**	T_COTS, T_COTS_ORD
rcv	successful return of **t_rcv**	T_COTS, T_COTS_ORD
rcvdis1	successful return of **t_rcvdis** with **ocnt** <= 0	T_COTS, T_COTS_ORD
rcvdis2	successful return of **t_rcvdis** with *ocnt* == 1	T_COTS, T_COTS_ORD
rcvdis3	successful return of **t_rcvdis** with *ocnt* > 1	T_COTS, T_COTS_ORD
rcvrel	successful return of **t_rcvrel**	T_COTS_ORD
rcvudata	successful return of **t_rcvudata**	T_CLTS
rcvuderr	successful return of **t_rcvuderr**	T_CLTS
pass_conn	receive a passed connection	T_COTS, T_COTS_ORD

Figure A-3: Transport Interface Incoming Events

Transport User Actions

In the state tables that follow, some state transitions are accompanied by a list of actions the transport user must take. These actions are represented by the notation [*n*], where *n* is the number of the specific action as described below:

[1]   Set the count of outstanding connect indications to zero.

[2]   Increment the count of outstanding connect indications.

[3]   Decrement the count of outstanding connect indications.

[4]   Pass a connection to another transport endpoint as indicated in *t_accept*.

State Tables

The following tables describe the Transport Interface state transitions. Given a current state and an event, the transition to the next state is shown, as well as any actions that must be taken by the transport user (indicated by [*n*]). The state is that of the transport provider as seen by the transport user.

The contents of each box represent the next state, given the current state (column) and the current incoming or outgoing event (row). An empty box represents a state/event combination that is invalid. Along with the next state, each box may include an action list (as specified in the previous section). The transport user must take the specific actions in the order specified in the state table.

The following should be understood when studying the state tables:

■ The **t_close** routine is referenced in the state tables (see *closed* event in Figure A-2), but may be called from any state to close a transport endpoint. If **t_close** is called when a transport address is bound to an endpoint, the address will be unbound. Also, if **t_close** is called when the transport connection is still active, the connection will be aborted.

■ If a transport user issues a routine out of sequence, the transport provider will recognize this and the routine will fail, setting **t_errno** to TOUTSTATE. The state will not change.

■ If any other transport error occurs, the state will not change unless explicitly stated on the manual page for that routine. The exception to this is a TLOOK or TNODATA error on **t_connect**, as described in Figure A-2. The state tables assume correct use of the Transport Interface.

■ The support routines **t_getinfo**, **t_getstate**, **t_alloc**, **t_free**, **t_sync**, **t_look**, and **t_error** are excluded from the state tables because they do not affect the state.

A separate table is shown for common local management steps, data transfer in connectionless-mode, and connection-establishment/connection-release/data-transfer in connection-mode.

event \ state	T_UNINIT	T_UNBND	T_IDLE
opened	T_UNBND		
bind		T_IDLE [1]	
optmgmt			T_IDLE
unbind			T_UNBND
closed		T_UNINIT	

Figure A-4: Common Local Management State Table

event \ state	T_IDLE
sndudata	T_IDLE
rcvudata	T_IDLE
rcvuderr	T_IDLE

Figure A-5: Connectionless-Mode State Table

state / event	T_IDLE	T_OUTCON	T_INCON	T_DATAXFER	T_OUTREL	T_INREL
connect1	T_DATAXFER					
connect2	T_OUTCON					
rcvconnect		T_DATAXFER				
listen	T_INCON [2]		T_INCON [2]			
accept1			T_DATAXFER[3]			
accept2			T_IDLE [3][4]			
accept3			T_INCON [3][4]			
snd				T_DATAXFER		T_INREL
rcv				T_DATAXFER	T_OUTREL	
snddis1		T_IDLE	T_IDLE [3]	T_IDLE	T_IDLE	T_IDLE
snddis2			T_INCON [3]			
rcvdis1		T_IDLE		T_IDLE	T_IDLE	T_IDLE
rcvdis2			T_IDLE [3]			
rcvdis3			T_INCON [3]			
sndrel				T_OUTREL		T_IDLE
rcvrel				T_INREL	T_IDLE	
pass_conn	T_DATAXFER					

Figure A-6: Connection-Mode State Table

B   Appendix B: Protocol Independence

Appendix B: Guidelines for Protocol

By defining a set of services common to many transport protocols, the Transport Interface offers protocol independence for user software. However, all transport protocols do not support all the services supported by the Transport Interface. If software must be run in a variety of protocol environments, only the common services should be accessed. The following guidelines highlight services that may not be common to all transport protocols.

■ In the connection-mode service, the concept of a transport service data unit (TSDU) may not be supported by all transport providers. The user should make no assumptions about the preservation of logical data boundaries across a connection. If messages must be transferred over a connection, a protocol should be implemented above the Transport Interface to support message boundaries.

■ Protocol- and implementation-specific service limits are returned by the **t_open** and **t_getinfo** routines. These limits are useful when allocating buffers to store protocol-specific transport addresses and options. It is the responsibility of the user to access these limits and then adhere to the limits throughout the communication process.

■ User data should not be transmitted with connect requests or disconnect requests [see *t_connect*(3N) and *t_snddis*(3N)]. Not all transport protocols support this capability.

■ The buffers in the **t_call** structure used for **t_listen** must be large enough to hold any information passed by the client during connection establishment. The server should use the T_ALL argument to **t_alloc**, which will determine the maximum buffer sizes needed to store the address, options, and user data for the current transport provider.

■ The user program should not look at or change options that are associated with any Transport Interface routine. These options are specific to the underlying transport protocol. The user should choose not to pass options with **t_connect** or **t_sndudata**. In such cases, the transport provider will use default values. Also, a server should use the options returned by **t_listen** when accepting a connection.

■ Protocol-specific addressing issues should be hidden from the user program. A client should not specify any protocol address on **t_bind**, but instead should allow the transport provider to assign an appropriate address to the transport endpoint. Similarly, a server should retrieve its address for **t_bind** in such a way that it does not require knowledge of the transport provider's address space. Such addresses should not be hard-coded into a program. A name server mechanism could be useful in this scenario, but the details for providing such a service are outside the scope of the Transport Interface.

■ The reason codes associated with **t_rcvdis** are protocol-dependent. The user should not interpret this information if protocol independence is a concern.

■ The error codes associated with **t_rcvuderr** are protocol-dependent. The user should not interpret this information if protocol independence is a concern.

■ The names of devices should not be hard-coded into programs, because the device node identifies a particular transport provider and is not protocol-independent.

■ The optional orderly release facility of the connection-mode service (provided by **t_sndrel** and **t_rcvrel**) should not be used by programs targeted for multiple protocol environments. This facility is not supported by all connection-based transport protocols. In particular, its use will prevent programs from successfully communicating with ISO open systems.

C   **Appendix C: Examples**

Appendix C: Examples

The examples presented throughout this guide are shown in entirety in this appendix.

Connection-Mode Client

The following code represents the connection-mode client program described in Chapter 3. This client establishes a transport connection with a server, and then receives data from the server and writes it to its standard output. The connection is released using the orderly release facility of the Transport Interface. This client will communicate with each of the connection-mode servers presented in the guide.

```c
#include <stdio.h>
#include <tiuser.h>
#include <fcntl.h>

#define SRV_ADDR    1    /* server's well-known address */

main( )
{
    int fd;
    int nbytes;
    int flags = 0;
    char buf[1024];
    struct t_call *sndcall;
    extern int t_errno;

    if ((fd = t_open("/dev/tivc", O_RDWR, NULL)) < 0) {
        t_error("t_open failed");
        exit(1);
    }

    if (t_bind(fd, NULL, NULL) < 0) {
        t_error("t_bind failed");
        exit(2);
    }

    /*
     * By assuming that the address is an integer value,
     * this program may not run over another protocol.
```

continued

```
 */
if ((sndcall = (struct t_call *)t_alloc(fd, T_CALL, T_ADDR)) == NULL) {
    t_error("t_alloc failed");
    exit(3);
}
sndcall->addr.len = sizeof(int);
*(int *)sndcall->addr.buf = SRV_ADDR;

if (t_connect(fd, sndcall, NULL) < 0) {
    t_error("t_connect failed for fd");
    exit(4);
}

while ((nbytes = t_rcv(fd, buf, 1024, &flags)) != -1) {
    if (fwrite(buf, 1, nbytes, stdout) < 0) {
        fprintf(stderr, "fwrite failed0);
        exit(5);
    }
}

if ((t_errno == TLOOK) && (t_look(fd) == T_ORDREL)) {
    if (t_rcvrel(fd) < 0) {
        t_error("t_rcvrel failed");
        exit(6);
    }
    if (t_sndrel(fd) < 0) {
        t_error("t_sndrel failed");
        exit(7);
    }
    exit(0);
}
t_error("t_rcv failed");
exit(8);
}
```

Connection-Mode Server

The following code represents the connection-mode server program described in Chapter 3. This server establishes a transport connection with a client, and then transfers a log file to the client on the other side of the connection. The connection is released using the orderly release facility of the Transport Interface. The connection-mode client presented earlier will communicate with this server.

```c
#include <tiuser.h>
#include <stropts.h>
#include <fcntl.h>
#include <stdio.h>
#include <signal.h>

#define DISCONNECT -1
#define SRV_ADDR    1  /* server's well-known address */

int conn_fd;           /* connection established here */
extern int t_errno;

main( )
{
    int listen_fd;     /* listening transport endpoint */
    struct t_bind *bind;
    struct t_call *call;

    if ((listen_fd = t_open("/dev/tivc", O_RDWR, NULL)) < 0) {
        t_error("t_open failed for listen_fd");
        exit(1);
    }

    /*
     * By assuming that the address is an integer value,
     * this program may not run over another protocol.
     */
    if ((bind = (struct t_bind *)t_alloc(listen_fd, T_BIND, T_ALL)) == NULL) {
        t_error("t_alloc of t_bind structure failed");
        exit(2);
    }
    bind->qlen = 1;
    bind->addr.len = sizeof(int);
```

continued

```
    *(int *)bind->addr.buf = SRV_ADDR;

    if (t_bind(listen_fd, bind, bind) < 0) {
        t_error("t_bind failed for listen_fd");
        exit(3);
    }

    /*
     * Was the correct address bound?
     */
    if (*(int *)bind->addr.buf != SRV_ADDR) {
        fprintf(stderr, "t_bind bound wrong address0);
        exit(4);
    }

    if ((call = (struct t_call *)t_alloc(listen_fd, T_CALL, T_ALL)) == NULL) {
        t_error("t_alloc of t_call structure failed");
        exit(5);
    }

    while (1) {
        if (t_listen(listen_fd, call) < 0) {
            t_error("t_listen failed for listen_fd");
            exit(6);
        }

        if ((conn_fd = accept_call(listen_fd, call)) != DISCONNECT)
            run_server(listen_fd);
    }
}


accept_call(listen_fd, call)
int listen_fd;
struct t_call *call;
{
    int resfd;

    if ((resfd = t_open("/dev/tivc", O_RDWR, NULL)) < 0) {
        t_error("t_open for responding fd failed");
        exit(7);
    }
```

continued

```
    if (t_bind(resfd, NULL, NULL) < 0) {
        t_error("t_bind for responding fd failed");
        exit(8);
    }

    if (t_accept(listen_fd, resfd, call) < 0) {
        if (t_errno == TLOOK) {   /* must be a disconnect */
            if (t_rcvdis(listen_fd, NULL) < 0) {
                t_error("t_rcvdis failed for listen_fd");
                exit(9);
            }
            if (t_close(resfd) < 0) {
                t_error("t_close failed for responding fd");
                exit(10);
            }
            /* go back up and listen for other calls */
            return(DISCONNECT);
        }
        t_error("t_accept failed");
        exit(11);
    }
    return(resfd);
}


connrelease()
{
    /* conn_fd is global because needed here */
    if (t_look(conn_fd) == T_DISCONNECT) {
        fprintf(stderr, "connection aborted0);
        exit(12);
    }

    /* else orderly release indication - normal exit */
    exit(0);
}


run_server(listen_fd)
int listen_fd;
{
    int nbytes;
    FILE *logfp;         /* file pointer to log file */
```

continued

```
char buf[1024];

switch (fork( )) {

case -1:
    perror("fork failed");
    exit(20);

default:    /* parent */

    /* close conn_fd and then go up and listen again */
    if (t_close(conn_fd) < 0) {
        t_error("t_close failed for conn_fd");
        exit(21);
    }
    return;

case 0:    /* child */

    /* close listen_fd and do service */
    if (t_close(listen_fd) < 0) {
        t_error("t_close failed for listen_fd");
        exit(22);
    }
    if ((logfp = fopen("logfile", "r")) == NULL) {
        perror("cannot open logfile");
        exit(23);
    }

    signal(SIGPOLL, connrelease);
    if (ioctl(conn_fd, I_SETSIG, S_INPUT) < 0) {
        perror("ioctl I_SETSIG failed");
        exit(24);
    }
    if (t_look(conn_fd) != 0) { /* was disconnect already there? */
        fprintf(stderr, "t_look returned unexpected event0);
        exit(25);
    }

    while ((nbytes = fread(buf, 1, 1024, logfp)) > 0)
        if (t_snd(conn_fd, buf, nbytes, 0) < 0) {
            t_error("t_snd failed");
            exit(26);
```

continued

```
    }

if (t_sndrel(conn_fd) < 0) {
    t_error("t_sndrel failed");
    exit(27);
}
pause( );    /* until orderly release indication arrives */
}
}
```

Connectionless-Mode Transaction Server

The following code represents the connectionless-mode transaction server program described in Chapter 4. This server waits for incoming datagram queries and then processes each query and sends a response.

```
#include <stdio.h>
#include <fcntl.h>
#include <tiuser.h>

#define SRV_ADDR   2        /* server's well-known address */

main( )
{
    int fd;
    int flags;
    struct t_bind *bind;
    struct t_unitdata *ud;
    struct t_uderr *uderr;
    extern int t_errno;


    if ((fd = t_open("/dev/tidg", O_RDWR, NULL)) < 0) {
        t_error("unable to open /dev/provider");
        exit(1);
    }

    if ((bind = (struct t_bind *)t_alloc(fd, T_BIND, T_ADDR)) == NULL) {
        t_error("t_alloc of t_bind structure failed");
        exit(2);
    }
    bind->addr.len = sizeof(int);
    *(int *)bind->addr.buf = SRV_ADDR;
    bind->qlen = 0;

    if (t_bind(fd, bind, bind) < 0) {
        t_error("t_bind failed");
        exit(3);
    }

    /*
     * is the bound address correct?
     */
```

continued

```
if (*(int *)bind->addr.buf != SRV_ADDR) {
    fprintf(stderr, "t_bind bound wrong address0);
    exit(4);
}

if ((ud = (struct t_unitdata *)t_alloc(fd, T_UNITDATA, T_ALL)) == NULL) {
    t_error("t_alloc of t_unitdata structure failed");
    exit(5);
}
if ((uderr = (struct t_uderr *)t_alloc(fd, T_UDERROR, T_ALL)) == NULL) {
    t_error("t_alloc of t_uderr structure failed");
    exit(6);
}

while (1) {
    if (t_rcvudata(fd, ud, &flags) < 0) {
        if (t_errno == TLOOK) {
            /*
             * Error on previously sent datagram
             */
            if (t_rcvuderr(fd, uderr) < 0) {
                t_error("t_rcvuderr failed");
                exit(7);
            }
            fprintf(stderr, "bad datagram, error = %d0,
                uderr->error);
            continue;
        }
        t_error("t_rcvudata failed");
        exit(8);
    }

    /*
     * Query( ) processes the request and places the
     * response in ud->udata.buf, setting ud->udata.len
     */
    query(ud);

    if (t_sndudata(fd, ud, 0) < 0) {
        t_error("t_sndudata failed");
        exit(9);
    }
}
```

continued

```
}

query( )
{
    /* Merely a stub for simplicity */
}
```

Read/Write Client

The following code represents the connection-mode **read/write** client program described in Chapter 5. This client establishes a transport connection
with a server, and then uses **cat** to retrieve the data sent by the server and
write it to its standard output. This client will communicate with each of the
connection-mode servers presented in the guide.

```
#include <stdio.h>
#include <tiuser.h>
#include <fcntl.h>
#include <stropts.h>

#define SRV_ADDR    1    /* server's well-known address */

main( )
{
    int fd;
    int nbytes;
    int flags = 0;
    char buf[1024];
    struct t_call *sndcall;
    extern int t_errno;

    if ((fd = t_open("/dev/tivc", O_RDWR, NULL)) < 0) {
        t_error("t_open failed");
        exit(1);
    }

    if (t_bind(fd, NULL, NULL) < 0) {
        t_error("t_bind failed");
        exit(2);
    }

    /*
     * By assuming that the address is an integer value,
     * this program may not run over another protocol.
     */

    if ((sndcall = (struct t_call *)t_alloc(fd, T_CALL, T_ADDR)) == NULL) {
        t_error("t_alloc failed");
        exit(3);
    }
```

continued

```
sndcall->addr.len = sizeof(int);
*(int *)sndcall->addr.buf = SRV_ADDR;

if (t_connect(fd, sndcall, NULL) < 0) {
    t_error("t_connect failed for fd");
    exit(4);
}

if (ioctl(fd, I_PUSH, "tirdwr") < 0) {
    perror("I_PUSH of tirdwr failed");
    exit(5);
}

close(0);
dup(fd);

execl("/bin/cat", "/bin/cat", 0);

perror("execl of /bin/cat failed");
exit(6);
}
```

Event-Driven Server

The following code represents the connection-mode server program described in Chapter 6. This server manages multiple connect indications in an event-driven manner. Either connection-mode client presented earlier will communicate with this server.

```c
#include <tiuser.h>
#include <fcntl.h>
#include <stdio.h>
#include <poll.h>
#include <stropts.h>
#include <signal.h>

#define NUM_FDS          1
#define MAX_CONN_IND   4
#define SRV_ADDR         1        /* server's well-known address */

int conn_fd;                      /* server connection here */
struct t_call *calls[NUM_FDS][MAX_CONN_IND];/* holds connect indications */
extern int t_errno;

main( )
{
    struct pollfd pollfds[NUM_FDS];
    struct t_bind *bind;
    int i;

    /*
     * Only opening and binding one transport endpoint,
     * but more could be supported
     */
    if ((pollfds[0].fd = t_open("/dev/tivc", O_RDWR, NULL)) < 0) {
        t_error("t_open failed");
        exit(1);
    }

    if ((bind = (struct t_bind *)t_alloc(pollfds[0].fd, T_BIND, T_ALL)) == NULL) {
        t_error("t_alloc of t_bind structure failed");
        exit(2);
    }
    bind->qlen = MAX_CONN_IND;
    bind->addr.len = sizeof(int);
```

continued

```
*(int *)bind->addr.buf = SRV_ADDR;

if (t_bind(pollfds[0].fd, bind, bind) < 0) {
   t_error("t_bind failed");
   exit(3);
}

/*
 * Was the correct address bound?
 */
if (*(int *)bind->addr.buf != SRV_ADDR) {
   fprintf(stderr, "t_bind bound wrong address0);
   exit(4);
}

pollfds[0].events = POLLIN;

while (1) {
   if (poll(pollfds, NUM_FDS, -1) < 0) {
      perror("poll failed");
      exit(5);
   }

   for (i = 0; i < NUM_FDS; i++) {

      switch (pollfds[i].revents) {

      default:
         perror("poll returned error event");
         exit(6);

      case 0:
         continue;

      case POLLIN:
         do_event(i, pollfds[i].fd);
         service_conn_ind(i, pollfds[i].fd);
      }
   }
 }
}
```

continued

```
do_event(slot, fd)
{
  struct t_discon *discon;
  int i;

  switch (t_look(fd)) {

  default:
    fprintf(stderr,"t_look returned an unexpected event0);
    exit(7);

  case T_ERROR:
    fprintf(stderr,"t_look returned T_ERROR event0);
    exit(8);

  case -1:
    t_error("t_look failed");
    exit(9);

  case 0:
    /* since POLLIN returned, this should not happen */
    fprintf(stderr,"t_look returned no event0);
    exit(10);

  case T_LISTEN:
    /*
     * find free element in calls array
     */
    for (i = 0; i < MAX_CONN_IND; i++) {
      if (calls[slot][i] == NULL)
          break;
    }

    if ((calls[slot][i] = (struct t_call *)t_alloc(fd, T_CALL, T_ALL)) == NULL)
    {
      t_error("t_alloc of t_call structure failed");
      exit(11);
    }

    if (t_listen(fd, calls[slot][i]) < 0) {
      t_error("t_listen failed");
      exit(12);
    }
```

continued

```
        break;

    case T_DISCONNECT:
      discon = (struct t_discon *)t_alloc(fd, T_DIS, T_ALL);

      if (t_rcvdis(fd, discon) < 0) {
        t_error("t_rcvdis failed");
        exit(13);
      }
      /*
       * find call ind in array and delete it
       */
      for (i = 0; i < MAX_CONN_IND; i++) {
        if (discon->sequence == calls[slot][i]->sequence) {
          t_free(calls[slot][i], T_CALL);
          calls[slot][i] = NULL;
        }
      }
      t_free(discon, T_DIS);
      break;
    }
}


service_conn_ind(slot, fd)
{
  int i;

  for (i = 0; i < MAX_CONN_IND; i++) {
    if (calls[slot][i] == NULL)
        continue;

    if ((conn_fd = t_open("/dev/tivc", O_RDWR, NULL)) < 0) {
      t_error("open failed");
      exit(14);
    }
    if (t_bind(conn_fd, NULL, NULL) < 0) {
      t_error("t_bind failed");
      exit(15);
    }

    if (t_accept(fd, conn_fd, calls[slot][i]) < 0) {
      if (t_errno == TLOOK) {
```

continued

```
            t_close(conn_fd);
            return;
        }
        t_error("t_accept failed");
        exit(16);
    }
    t_free(calls[slot][i], T_CALL);
    calls[slot][i] = NULL;

    run_server(fd);
  }
}


connrelease( )
{
  /* conn_fd is global because needed here */
  if (t_look(conn_fd) == T_DISCONNECT) {
    fprintf(stderr, "connection aborted0);
    exit(12);
  }

  /* else orderly release indication - normal exit */
  exit(0);
}


run_server(listen_fd)
int listen_fd;
{
  int nbytes;
  FILE *logfp;      /* file pointer to log file */
  char buf[1024];

  switch (fork( )) {

  case -1:
    perror("fork failed");
    exit(20);

  default: /* parent */

    /* close conn_fd and then go up and listen again */
```

continued

```
    if (t_close(conn_fd) < 0) {
        t_error("t_close failed for conn_fd");
        exit(21);
    }
    return;

case 0:      /* child */

    /* close listen_fd and do service */
    if (t_close(listen_fd) < 0) {
        t_error("t_close failed for listen_fd");
        exit(22);
    }
    if ((logfp = fopen("logfile", "r")) == NULL) {
        perror("cannot open logfile");
        exit(23);
    }

    signal(SIGPOLL, connrelease);
    if (ioctl(conn_fd, I_SETSIG, S_INPUT) < 0) {
        perror("ioctl I_SETSIG failed");
        exit(24);
    }
    if (t_look(conn_fd) != 0) {/* was disconnect already there? */
        fprintf(stderr, "t_look returned unexpected event0);
        exit(25);
    }

    while ((nbytes = fread(buf, 1, 1024, logfp)) > 0)
        if (t_snd(conn_fd, buf, nbytes, 0) < 0) {
            t_error("t_snd failed");
            exit(26);
        }

    if (t_sndrel(conn_fd) < 0) {
        t_error("t_sndrel failed");
        exit(27);
    }
    pause( );  /* until orderly release indication arrives */
    }
}
```

Glossary

The following terms apply to the Transport Interface:

Abortive release   An abrupt termination of a transport connection, which may result in the loss of data.

Asynchronous execution

The mode of execution in which Transport Interface routines will never block while waiting for specific asynchronous events to occur, but instead will return immediately if the event is not pending.

Client   The transport user in connection-mode that initiates the establishment of a transport connection.

Connection establishment

The phase in connection-mode that enables two transport users to create a transport connection between them.

Connection-mode   A circuit-oriented mode of transfer in which data is passed from one user to another over an established connection in a reliable, sequenced manner.

Connectionless-mode

A mode of transfer in which data is passed from one user to another in self-contained units with no logical relationship required among multiple units.

Connection release

The phase in connection-mode that terminates a previously established transport connection between two users.

Datagram   A unit of data transferred between two users of the connectionless-mode service.

Data transfer   The phase in connection-mode or connectionless-mode that supports the transfer of data between two transport users.

Expedited data   Data that is considered urgent. The specific semantics of *expedited data* are defined by the transport protocol that provides the transport service.

Expedited transport service data unit
The amount of expedited user data, the identity of which is preserved from one end of a transport connection to the other (that is, an expedited message).

Local management
The phase in either connection-mode or connectionless-mode in which a transport user establishes a transport endpoint and binds a transport address to the endpoint. Functions in this phase perform local operations and require no transport layer traffic over the network.

Orderly release
A procedure for gracefully terminating a transport connection with no loss of data.

Peer user
The user with whom a given user is communicating above the Transport Interface.

Server
The transport user in connection-mode that offers services to other users (clients) and enables these clients to establish a transport connection to it.

Service indication
The notification of a pending event generated by the provider to a user of a particular service.

Service primitive
The unit of information passed across a service interface that contains either a service request or service indication.

Service request
A request for some action generated by a user to the provider of a particular service.

Synchronous execution
The mode of execution in which Transport Interface routines may block while waiting for specific asynchronous events to occur.

Transport address
The identifier used to differentiate and locate specific transport endpoints in a network.

Transport connection

The communication circuit that is established between two transport users in connection-mode.

Transport endpoint

The local communication channel between a transport user and a transport provider.

Transport Interface

The library routines and state transition rules that support the services of a transport protocol.

Transport provider

The transport protocol that provides the services of the Transport Interface.

Transport service data unit

The amount of user data whose identity is preserved from one end of a transport connection to the other (that is, a message).

Transport user The user-level application or protocol that accesses the services of the Transport Interface.

Virtual circuit A transport connection established in connection-mode.

The following acronyms are used throughout this guide:

CLTS Connectionless Transport Service

COTS Connection Oriented Transport Service

ETSDU Expedited Transport Service Data Unit

TSDU Transport Service Data Unit

Index

7713